insight text guide

Lisa Fletcher

Girl with a Pearl Earring

Tracy Chevalier

First published in 2010. Reprinted 2012, 2016, 2020, 2023.

Insight Publications Pty Ltd
3/350 Charman Road
Cheltenham VIC 3192
Australia
Tel: +61 3 8571 4950
Fax: +61 3 8571 0257
Email: books@insightpublications.com.au

www.insightpublications.com.au

National Library of Australia Cataloguing-in-Publication entry:
Fletcher, Lisa Girl with a Pearl Earring: text guide
For secondary and tertiary students.
ISBN 9781875882724
1. Chevalier, Tracy
(Series : Insight text guide)

Other ISBNs:
9781922525024 (digital)
9781922525017 (bundle: print + digital)

Cover design by Gisela Beer, based on a concept by The Modern Art Production Group

Printed by Markono Print Media Pte Ltd

contents

CHARACTER MAP

INTRODUCTION

Tracy Chevalier's historical novel, *Girl with a Pearl Earring,* is named after a painting by the famous seventeenth-century Dutch artist, Johannes Vermeer. She has owned a poster of the painting – often called the 'Dutch Mona Lisa' – since she was nineteen years old. On the novel's website, Chevalier says, *'I have always loved Vermeer's paintings* ... There is so much mystery in each painting, in the women he depicts, so many stories suggested but not told. I wanted to tell one of them'.

Chevalier's story is one of five recent novels that take their inspiration from the work of Vermeer and other seventeenth-century Dutch painters. Deborah Moggach's *Tulip Fever,* Susan Vreeland's *Girl in Hyacinth Blue,* Katherine Weber's *The Music Lesson,* Gregory Maguire's *Confessions of an Ugly Stepsister* and Chevalier's novel were all published within two years of each other. Read in this context, this text invites us to consider the value and the appeal of Vermeer's paintings to writers and readers today – 330 years after his death. The popularity of these historical fictions – Chevalier's novel was an immediate bestseller – demonstrates the continuing relevance of stories of the distant past to our lives in the present.

Girl with a Pearl Earring tells the story of the young woman depicted in the painting reproduced on the novel's cover. Art historians speculate that one of Vermeer's daughters may have been the model for his painting. Instead, Chevalier imagines her as an outsider in the artist's household: a sixteen-year-old girl, Griet, who leaves her family home to become Vermeer's maid. Chevalier uses what little is known about Vermeer's life as the basis for her powerful tale about the way in which individuals are defined by their difference from others. History provides the setting for fiction. This novel makes us think carefully about the relationship between fact and fiction, truth and lies, what we can and can't know.

In many ways this is a novel about secrecy. Just as the characters in the novel keep secrets from each other, so too Vermeer's painting keeps its secret. We may never know who the girl *really* was, but as this novel attests, there is a great deal of pleasure in imagining who she might have been. Of the novel, Chevalier has said: 'I didn't want it to be about Vermeer, I wanted it to be about [the girl]. She would have a voice and a story, which she hadn't ever had' (quoted in Librie 2011).

This engaging and intelligent novel can be studied from multiple perspectives. Use the material in this guide to develop your own critical responses to it.

BACKGROUND & CONTEXT

This chapter provides background information about Vermeer and his historical period. It is important that you do further research. However, be careful not to get bogged down in historical detail. Instead, use your research to enrich your analysis of *Girl with a Pearl Earring*. Study the paintings featured in the novel closely. In a glowing review, Deborah Moggach (1999) writes: 'It is deeply revealing about the process of painting and is best read with a volume of Vermeer's paintings open beside you – it then becomes a truly magical experience'. The websites and texts listed at the end of this guide are a good starting point. You'll find excellent reproductions of all of Vermeer's paintings on the web.

Seventeenth-century Delft, the Netherlands

The Netherlands (also known as Holland) is a country in north-western Europe, bordered by the North Sea, Germany and Belgium. Its capital city is Amsterdam; however, its government is based in The Hague. The adjective for the Netherlands is 'Dutch'.

The novel is set in a period of Dutch history known as the 'Dutch Golden Age' (c. 1609–1702/13). The seventeenth century (1600–1700) was a time of economic prosperity and political success for the Dutch. Dutch artists flourished. After Rembrandt, Vermeer is widely considered to be the best artist of this period and he is certainly one of the most famous. Other seventeenth-century Dutch artists include Pieter de Hooch (1629–1684), Gerard ter Borch (1617–1681) and Jan Steen (c. 1625–1679).

Chevalier's story is set in Delft, a city in the west of the Netherlands, which was an important European trade centre in the sixteenth and seventeenth centuries. When Vermeer was born in 1632, approximately 25,000 people lived in Delft. The city was best known for its blue and white glazed earthenware ('Delftware'). In the novel, this is the industry in which Griet's father works and in which her brother spends his unhappy apprenticeship.

Vermeer scholar Arthur K Wheelock Jr (1995) writes:

> By the seventeenth century Delft was already a venerable city with a long and distinguished past. The walls and medieval gates of Vermeer's native city, visible in his remarkable *View of Delft* ... had controlled traffic over land and water and provided defence for more than three centuries. (p.15)

During the seventeenth century Delft's prosperity and its beauty made it a popular travel destination. One of the city's greatest attractions was the New Church, visible from the house on the Oude Langendijck where most of the novel's action takes place:

> From the front of the house the New Church tower was visible just across the canal. A strange view for a Catholic family, I thought. A church they will never even go inside. (p.16)

Griet attends a service at this church early in the novel (p.69). Griet is a Protestant girl who goes to work in a Catholic household. In the mid-seventeenth century, approximately eighty per cent of Delft's inhabitants were Protestant. (They made up about two-thirds of the Netherlands' population.) Simon Schama, in his book about the Dutch Golden Age (which Chevalier read as part of her research), writes that the Catholic minority had an 'existence on sufferance' (p.57); they were tolerated but looked down upon. The grand New Church symbolised the power of Protestant religions in Delft and the Netherlands. Catholics were not allowed to worship publicly; they attended small private churches (known as 'hidden' churches). One of these was next door to Vermeer's mother-in-law's house in an area of Delft known as 'Papists Corner' because of the large number of Catholics living there.

Q Trace the references to religious difference in *Girl with a Pearl Earring*. According to the novel, how are Protestantism and Catholicism different? How do Griet's family's values and beliefs differ from those of Vermeer and his family?

Johannes Vermeer (1632–1675)

In preparation for writing *Girl with a Pearl Earring,* Chevalier read John Michael Montias' excellent book, *Vermeer and his Milieu* (1989). He writes:

> In spite of all of my efforts and of those who preceded me in combing through Delft's archives, less documentary evidence has survived regarding Vermeer himself than regarding his grandparents, his uncles and aunts, and especially his in-laws: Maria Thins, the formidable mother of his wife Catharina, and Catharina's irascible brother Willem. Vermeer seems to have been exclusively devoted to his art … There is little to go on to reconstruct his personality, beyond his ability to get along with a very domineering and contentious mother-in-law. (p.xv)

That we know so little about Vermeer is one of his attractions for fiction writers. Chevalier used facts as the basis for fiction. That the 'facts' of Vermeer's life are still the subject of debate meant that she was able to imagine the story behind the painting without worrying too much about getting the facts straight. For example, Montias believes that Pieter van Ruijven was probably Vermeer's patron – as he is in the novel – but other historians argue that there is no basis for Montias' claim.

Relevant information about Vermeer's life:

- 1632: Born in Delft, baptised in New Church (Protestant).
- Little is known about his life between his baptism and his marriage. During his late childhood and adolescence it's most likely that he lived at his parents' inn in Delft, the 'Mechelen'.
- Probably completed a six-year painting apprenticeship during this time, perhaps in another Dutch city.
- 1653: Converted to Catholicism and married Catharina Bolnes, a woman from a well-off family.

- 1653: Joined Guild of Saint Luke as a master painter, but evidence suggests that he painted too slowly to earn his living from painting. He served as its headman twice. In the novel, Griet comes to work for Vermeer because her father is also a Guild member.
- Made some money by trading paintings, but probably devoted little time to this activity (see p.17).
- Inherited the 'Mechelen' after his mother's death in 1670, but this made little difference to his income. It appears that he was financially dependent on his mother-in-law, Maria Thins, who owned the house where he lived for at least the last sixteen years of his life.
- Most of the documents mentioning Vermeer that survive today relate to his financial status. We know, for example, that in 1657 he borrowed two hundred guilders from Pieter Claesz van Ruijven, a wealthy citizen of Delft. This record, together with evidence that van Ruijven's daughter owned a substantial number of Vermeer's paintings, has led to speculation that van Ruijven was Vermeer's patron. He plays a central role in Chevalier's novel.
- Hendrick van Buyten, a baker in Delft, purchased a number of Vermeer's paintings. Catharina also gave him two paintings after Vermeer's death as payment for a debt (see p.245). The baker in Chevalier's novel is based on van Buyten.
- Eleven children survived infancy: Mary (Maertge in the novel), Elisabeth (Lisbeth), Cornelia, Aleydis, Beatrix, Johannes, Gertruyd, Franciscus, Catharina, Ignatius and an unidentified child. Cornelia plays the largest role in the novel.
- Close analysis of Vermeer's paintings (composition, perspective, precise detail) has led historians to speculate that he may have used a camera obscura to assist his painting (a lens in a box/cubicle used to project an image onto a screen). While there is no documentary evidence to support this claim, Vermeer's association with Antony van Leeuwenhoek, the inventor of the microscope and other optical instruments, suggests that he possibly had access to such a device. Van Leeuwenhoek was the executor of Vermeer's will.

- Died 1675, aged forty-three. Catharina claimed his death was the result of the family's financial decline. In his later years, Vermeer found it almost impossible to sell paintings, because of the negative impact of the war between the Netherlands and France on the art market. The war also reduced Maria Thins' income and the family fell increasingly into debt. After his death, Catharina said:

> Johannes Vermeer, during the ruinous and protracted war was not only unable to sell any of his art but also, to his great detriment, was left sitting with the paintings of other masters that he was dealing in, as a result of which and owing to the great burden of his children, having nothing of his own, he had lapsed into such decay and decadence, which he had taken so to heart that, as if he had fallen into a frenzy, in a day and a half he had gone from being healthy to being dead. (quoted in Montias 1989, p.351)

Vermeer's paintings

Vermeer mostly painted intimate domestic scenes, often featuring a woman alone – lace-making, pouring milk, writing a letter. He also painted religious scenes, streetscapes and a few 'tronien', including *Girl with a Pearl Earring*. (Note: Troni is a style of Dutch painting that depicts close-up head-and-shoulders pictures of individuals in character dress.)

Only thirty-five paintings by Vermeer survive. It is not known who modelled for him, but research suggests that Vermeer included rooms, furniture and objects from his immediate surroundings in his paintings. Chevalier mentions several of these: Catharina's yellow mantle; the box in *A Lady Writing*; the lions-head chairs; the gilded jug; paintings owned by Maria Thins. Most of the paintings were probably completed in the same room: his first floor studio in Maria Thins' house.

Girl with a Pearl Earring (c.1665–66)

A major exhibition of Vermeer's work was held at the National Gallery of Art, Washington and The Royal Cabinet of Paintings, Mauritshuis, The

Hague in 1995–96. It was enormously successful and partly explains the resurgence of interest in Vermeer and his historical period. In the exhibition catalogue, art historian Arthur K Wheelock Jr (1995) describes this extraordinarily beautiful painting:

> As this young girl stares out at the viewer with liquid eyes and parted mouth, she radiates purity, captivating all that gaze upon her. Her soft, smooth skin is as unblemished as the surface of her large, teardrop-shaped pearl earring. Like a vision emanating from the darkness, she belongs to no specific time or place. Her exotic turban, wrapping her head in crystalline blue, is surmounted by a striking yellow fabric that falls dramatically behind her shoulder, lending an air of mystery to the image. (p.166)

Chevalier attended the exhibition at Mauritshuis where she first saw Vermeer's original painting. In her novel, Griet never has the opportunity to look closely at the finished painting. It is only described once:

> The painting was like none of his others. It was just of me, of my head and shoulders, with no tables or curtains, no windows or powderbrushes to soften and distract. He had painted me with my eyes wide, the light falling across my face but the left side of me in shadow. I was wearing blue and yellow and brown. The cloth wound round my head made me look not like myself, but like Griet from another town, even from another country altogether. The background was black, making me appear very much alone, although I was clearly looking at someone. I seemed to be waiting for something I did not think would ever happen. (pp.202–03)

Other paintings featured in the novel

- *View of Delft* (c.1660–61). Reproduced on novel's cover. Griet and her father discuss it early in the novel (p.7).
- *Woman with a Pearl Necklace* (c.1664). The first painting Griet sees in Vermeer's studio (pp.37–8 and 50).
- *The Milkmaid* (c.1658–60). Like Montias, Chevalier suggests Vermeer's servant, Tanneke, may have been the model. See p.40 and pp.166–7.
- *The Girl with the Wineglass* (c.1659–60). Griet never sees this painting. Other characters refer to it as the painting of the 'maid with the red dress'. See pp.134–5 and p.169.
- *A Lady Writing* (Also called *Lady Writing a Letter*) (c.1665). Van Ruijven's wife models for this painting in the novel. This is the painting Griet 'changes'. See pp.135–44 and p.146.
- *Woman with a Lute* (c.1664). One very brief reference (p.137).
- *The Concert* (c.1665–66). Van Ruijven, his daughter and his sister sit for it in the novel. See pp.179, 184 and 201.
- *Young Woman with a Water Pitcher* (also called *Woman with a Wine Jug*) (c.1664–65). See pp.95–7 and 106–08.
- *The Procuress* by Dirck van Baburen (1590/1595–1624). Owned by Maria Thins. Vermeer included it in the background of *The Concert* and *A Lady Seated at the Virginal* (not mentioned in the novel). Griet bases the headdress she wears for Vermeer's painting of her on the turban worn by the old woman in *The Procuress* (p.193). Also pp.179 and 218.

GENRE, STRUCTURE AND STYLE

Genre

Historical novel

Girl with a Pearl Earring is an historical novel: a long narrative prose fiction set in the past. Historical novels take their settings and some of their characters and events from history. Tracy Chevalier read widely about Vermeer's life and seventeenth-century Delft. Historical facts are scattered throughout the novel, but they do not interrupt the flow of the fictional story. Chevalier says: 'I'm a novelist first and the history – it's really fun, and fun to research – is really secondary' (quoted in Grant 2001). One reviewer, Gary Schwartz (2001) accuses all five of the recent novels published about Vermeer of being historically inaccurate. He writes that Chevalier and the other authors share a 'mistaken view of ... Vermeer and his historic Dutch context.' He argues, for instance, that Chevalier's portrayal of religious difference is simplistic because Griet refers to herself as a 'Protestant': 'Griet would have belonged to a congregation that called itself 'Christian' and that distinguished itself from other Protestant churches even more emphatically than Catholics' (p.104). Vermeer's patron, for example, would have belonged to a different church than Griet.

Q How important is historical accuracy? Does it matter if Chevalier's description of seventeenth-century Dutch life isn't quite true to history?

Q What is the aim of *Girl with a Pearl Earring*? Is it written to educate us in some way (to teach us about Vermeer and his historical period, to demonstrate the value of his paintings) or was Chevalier's aim simply to entertain her readers by telling a compelling story (or does it do both things at once)? Did you enjoy *Girl with a Pearl Earring*? What did you learn from reading it?

Coming-of-age novel; bildungsroman

Girl with a Pearl Earring can also be classified as a 'coming-of-age novel' or bildungsroman. Bildungsroman is a German term used to describe novels which focus on the protagonist's transition from childhood through to maturity (*Bildung* = education; *Roman* = novel). See 'Themes, Ideas & Values'.

Structure

Girl with a Pearl Earring has four sections: three main sections and a shorter one that functions as an epilogue to the main narrative. The action takes place over three years and each section narrates the events of one year (1664, 1665, 1666). The fourth section is set ten years later (1676).

Key point

This is a very carefully structured novel; each stage of the story recalls what has come before and anticipates what is coming next. This happens in a number of ways: in the repetition of certain words; in the descriptions of characters; in the frequent use of key metaphors; in the links drawn between scenes or images; and, most obviously, in the moments when Griet directly comments on the significance of an event to her future.

Consider the relationship between the novel's structure and its key themes. Remember, for instance, that *Girl with a Pearl Earring* is about the transition from childhood to adulthood, about what it means to look forward as you are looking backwards. Early in the novel, Chevalier makes frequent use of foreshadowing to anticipate later events. A good example of this is the description of Griet's favourite tile (see 'Themes, Ideas & Values').

Q Try breaking down the novel for yourself. This will help you gain a better understanding of the novel's multi-layered plot. Draw a 'map' of the narrative (or a flowchart) on a large sheet of paper using arrows to indicate the relationship between scenes/events, to identify key scenes, to map how subplots relate to the main narrative (e.g. Griet's brother's story) and/or to trace Chevalier's use of repeated images (e.g. the vegetable circle, the spinning knife, the eight-pointed star).

First-person narration; focalisation

Key point

The novel is narrated in the first person ('I'). Griet is both its main protagonist and its narrator.

Griet tells her story in the past tense from an imagined point in the novel's future. We see everything through Griet's eyes; the novel is focalised through her. This encourages readers to identify with Griet and the difficulties she faces coming to terms with her place in the world. While the first-person narration draws us close to Griet, other aspects of the book make us aware of the distance between her world and ours. Be careful to distinguish between the author (Chevalier) and the narrator (Griet) when you are discussing this book. It's easy to confuse the two when reading a first-person narrative. While we only have direct access to Griet's point of view, Chevalier provides clues to alternative interpretations of events. For example, she uses dialogue to show the perspectives of other characters, e.g. van Leeuwenhoek (p.197).

Q How else does Chevalier give us clues that Griet's version of the story is not the only one?

Q One of the most important questions to consider when you are analysing this novel is the question of Griet's reliability. Is Griet a reliable or an unreliable narrator? Do you believe her interpretation of events and characters?

Style

Key point

Chevalier's writing style in this novel is an attempt to find a written equivalent to Vermeer's visual style.

We can see this in the novel's very detailed descriptions of people, objects and their spatial relationship to each other (composition), and in the close attention paid to the exact colours of things. Vermeer's paintings are celebrated for the way they 'capture a moment' on canvas – a girl pouring milk, a woman fastening her necklace. Chevalier seeks to do something similar with carefully written descriptions of moments in time, e.g. Catharina lying in bed with her newborn son; Tanneke scrubbing the tiles. Her writing makes us visualise the novel's action. Like Vermeer's paintings, Chevalier's novel delights in the details of everyday domestic life and invites us to linger on things we would not normally consider the subject of art: folding laundry, dusting surfaces, a butcher's bloody hands.

Q In both Vermeer's paintings and Chevalier's novel, everyday household objects are made to stand for something bigger; they have a symbolic significance. Make a list of the everyday items that feature significantly in the book, e.g. the ivory comb, a knife. What do they symbolise?

SECTION-BY-SECTION ANALYSIS

This section-by-section analysis provides a summary of *Girl with a Pearl Earring*. It highlights key scenes, traces the development of the plot and raises questions to help you prepare your own notes on the text. In order to make it more user-friendly, I've divided each major section of the novel into smaller parts (scenes/episodes or a number of scenes that work together) e.g. Catharina sees painting; Griet leaves household (pp.223–9).

Key point

Devise an effective method for taking and organising reading notes. One approach is to use a journal for scribbling your ideas and thoughts, then use a card file (or a computer database) to put them in order.

1664 (pp.1–92)

Summary: *Griet employed to clean Vermeer's studio; struggles to find her place in a strange household and to keep her family together (made more difficult by her father's blindness, Frans' unhappiness, and Agnes' death); attracts attention of Pieter the son, Vermeer and van Ruijven, and is increasingly attracted to Vermeer.*

Griet meets the Vermeers; the vegetable circle (pp.3–6)

- Functions as prologue to main action.
- Initiates suspense, draws us into the story.
- Introduces key themes: the different ways we 'look' at things; the relationship between art and everyday life; difference (class, religion, gender).
- Foreshadows roles Catharina and Vermeer play in Griet's life.
- Anticipates changes in Griet's relationship with her family (introduces Griet's mother and sister).
- Introduces visual images repeated throughout novel, e.g. vegetable circle, spinning knife.

Griet is chopping vegetables for soup when she hears a man and a woman arrive at the house and her mother showing them to the kitchen. The novel's first sentence signals that this visit will be a pivotal event in Griet's life: 'My mother did not tell me they were coming' (p.3). Griet recognises that the visitors are not the kind of people who usually come to her family's home: 'They were the kind of voices we heard rarely in our house. I could hear rich carpets in their voices, books and pearls and fur' (p.3). The description of her mother's voice ('a cooking pot, a flagon', p.3) reinforces this point.

Key point

The opening pages of the novel anticipate the extent to which Griet's family and the Vermeers will be defined in opposition to each other, most significantly by their difference of class (economic and social status) and religion (Protestant versus Catholic).

The descriptions of Vermeer and Catharina in this scene emphasise the fundamental difference between them. Catharina is clearly nervous and struggles to focus on the things around her. Her husband, by contrast, looks at things carefully as we learn by his close attention to Griet's circle of sliced vegetables (p.5). Vermeer asks her why she organises the vegetables by colour. Her response surprises him: 'The colours fight when they are side by side, sir' (p.5). This episode anticipates the link between Vermeer and Griet, which impacts heavily on both their lives: they share a heightened aesthetic sense, an appreciation of colour and composition, and the desire and ability to look closely at things and their relationship to each other. It promises also that Griet will not be the only one to learn something from their relationship.

After the couple leaves, Griet's mother tells her that she is to begin working as their maid the next day. Her mother drops the sliced vegetables into the soup pot: 'The pie slices I had made so carefully were ruined' (p.6). This moment marks the end of Griet's life as she knows it – the loss of the comforting harmony represented by the neat circle of colours – and the beginning of the next (and most difficult) stage of her life.

Griet's family; Frans (pp.7–10)

- Introduces Griet's blind father: continues emphasis on how characters 'see' things.
- *View of Delft.*
- Theme: growing up.

Griet goes upstairs to the attic to talk to her father, a tile painter who lost his sight and his trade when a kiln exploded. Griet learns that the visitors were Vermeer and his wife and that she has been employed to clean the painter's studio. This section of the novel highlights the value Griet places on her close relationship with her brother, Frans, and her sister, Agnes. Pay careful attention to how these relationships change throughout the novel. Agnes misses Frans, who has left home to be an apprentice tile painter. She is upset that Griet is leaving home. Griet reflects on the last time she saw Frans.

Griet leaves home; Vermeer's household; Griet slaps Cornelia (pp.10–24)

- Themes: growing up; the gaze; difference (Griet an outsider).
- 'Favourite tile'; eight-pointed star.
- Introduces Vermeer's household: the children, Tanneke, Maria Thins.

This is an important section of the novel, which describes Griet's experience of leaving one household (familiar, comforting) and entering another (strange, discomforting).

On the morning when she first leaves her family home, Griet's father presents her with her 'favourite tile': 'To remind you of home … Of us'. Read the description of this tile carefully (pp.10–11). It plays an important symbolic role in the novel (see 'Themes, Ideas & Values').

Griet thinks about Delft as she walks towards the Oude Langendijck. There is an eight-pointed star in the centre of the town square: 'Each point aimed towards a different part of Delft' (p.13). The significance of Griet's religious difference from the family she is to work for is highlighted here. 'Papists Corner' is the only part of the city Griet has never explored.

Griet's first impressions of the house also emphasise her discomfort with the Vermeers' Catholicism. We see this particularly in her reaction to religious paintings – of Christ on the Cross, of the Virgin Mary (see pp.17–18 and 20).

When Griet arrives at the house, the Vermeers' four daughters and their baby son (Maertge, Lisbeth, Cornelia, Aleydis, Johannes) are sitting outside. Cornelia's 'bright hair' (p.15) and her behaviour makes her stand out from the others: 'She will be a handful, I thought' (p.15). Griet meets Tanneke and feels immediately that their relationship will not be an easy one (p.17).

Tanneke takes Griet to meet Maria Thins. Importantly, Griet bases her first assessment of Maria Thins on how the older woman looks at her: 'Though she seemed to look at me casually, her gaze was watchful. When she narrowed her eyes I realised she knew everything I was thinking. I turned my head so that my cap hid my face' (p.18). Note that Griet's self-conscious gesture recalls the hidden face of the girl in her father's tile painting.

Key point

All of the adult characters introduced so far have been described in terms of the way they look at Griet.

Tanneke shows Griet the house and lists her duties: laundry, cleaning Vermeer's studio, shopping. This tour of the house emphasises Griet's discomfort. Griet senses that she will be alone in this house (the odd one out). She learns, for example, that she is to sleep in 'a hole in the floor of one of the storage rooms' (p.19).

Griet has her first altercation with Cornelia: Griet slaps Cornelia's face when she laughs at Griet's request for help carrying water from the canal to the laundry (p.22; also pp.225 and 247). When Griet returns to the canal to fetch the pot she had left behind, she sees it floating in the water. She guesses that Cornelia is responsible and turns her head 'so that the girls could not see [her] face' (p.23). A boatman helps her retrieve the pot. This is the same man who had called out to her earlier in the day:

'I merely nodded and lowered my head so that the edge of my cap hid my face' (p.12). Griet's meeting with the boatman links two of the novel's principal themes: what it means to be looked at, and the inequality of men and women. Griet's shyness before the man is tied to their sexual difference. By refusing to look at him earlier in the day, she had signalled her innocence, her sexual unavailability. His advances become bolder when she returns his gaze in this scene: 'Oh, you're looking at me now that you want something from me, are you? There's a change!' He tries to kiss her and she is forced to '[wrestle] the pot from him' (p.24). This scene forecasts the difficulties Griet will have avoiding being looked at by the men in the novel. It also begins to explain the difference between Griet's father's tile painting and Vermeer's 'tronien'. By the time Vermeer paints Griet, she no longer hides her face, as she does in her father's tile painting of her, but looks directly at the artist. It is therefore significant that, as she walks back towards the house, Griet thinks she sees 'movement' in the window of Vermeer's studio: 'I stared but could see nothing except the reflected sky' (p.24). This shift from her exchange with the boatman to thinking about her new master (wondering if he is watching her) is a subtle indication of the possibility that Griet will not always hide her face behind her cap.

The work of a maid; the butchers; the cellar (pp.24–32)

- Highlights difference between Griet and the Vermeers.

Tanneke, Griet and Maertge visit the Meat Hall. She is 'pleased to be in a familiar place' (p.27). Griet remembers that Frans 'had almost run away' from his apprenticeship, 'because he could not face the strangeness day after day' (p.28). At the end of her first day as a maid, she is 'exhausted' by the strain of being 'in a strange house where everything was new and I was always tense and serious' (p.31). At the Meat Hall Tanneke introduces Griet to the Vermeer's butcher: 'Pieter [the father] looked me over as if I were a plump chicken he was considering roasting' (p.28). The way the butcher looks at Griet is directly contrasted with the way Vermeer looks at her on the next page: 'I stood still and he paused, the light behind him so that I could not see his face. I did not know if he was looking down the hallway at me' (pp.29–30). The meal Griet eats that afternoon (p.30) shows the difference between Griet's family's fortunes and the Vermeers'. The importance of their religious difference is also illustrated – by Griet's uneasiness in the 'Crucifixion room' (p.31) and by her even greater discomfort when she sees the painting of Christ on the Cross that hangs at the foot of her bed.

Vermeer's studio; Maria Thins (pp.33–9)

- Similarities between Griet and Vermeer.
- *Woman with a Pearl Necklace.*

Vermeer's studio is the only room in the house that reminds Griet of home: 'The room gave off a clean, sharp odour of linseed oil that reminded me of the smell of my father's clothes when he had returned from the tile factory at night' (p.33). Unlike the rest of the house, her first impression of the studio is of its familiarity rather than its strangeness. It is also significant that Catharina does not enter the studio, but watches Griet from the doorway. Griet is surprised by her reflection in a mirror: 'I gazed at myself' (p.34). The image of Griet in the mirror foreshadows Vermeer's portrait of her: 'Although I had an anxious guilty expression, my face was also bathed in light, making my skin glow' (p.34).

Key point

The studio is described in detail; careful attention is paid to the objects in the room and to their placement as though the narrator is describing the composition of a painting.

Griet looks at the painting on the easel: *Woman with a Pearl Necklace* (pp.37–8).

Pieter the son; Vermeer (pp.39–47)

- *The Milkmaid.*
- Develops link between themes: what it means to be looked at; men and women; growing up.

Griet meets the butcher's 'handsome son' (p.41). Again, Griet focuses on how others look at her and at each other (p.42). The exchange of gazes in this scene – between Griet and the two men, between father and son – establishes Pieter's interest in Griet and foreshadows the key role he will play in her future: 'As I turned to go I caught the glance that passed between father and son. Even then I knew somehow what it meant, and what it would mean for me' (p.42).

Even though Griet has barely seen Vermeer, she is intensely aware of his presence in the house. When she does come 'face to face with him', she finds it 'hard to meet his eyes' (p.44). Vermeer's patron, van Ruijven, and his wife (Vermeer's model) arrive at the house. Griet's brief encounter with van Ruijven's wife is an important moment in the text: compare this face-to-face meeting with the one with Vermeer. Whereas she found it impossible to look at Vermeer, she stares openly at van Ruijven's wife, transfixed by the way she both looks like and unlike the woman in the painting (p.45). The next time Griet sees Vermeer, she again hides her face.

First visit home (pp.47–51)

- Agnes' loneliness.

Griet reveals, 'when I turned into my street I thought how different it felt already after less than a week away' (p.48). She finds herself keeping details about her new life from her family and finds it difficult to discuss Vermeer's painting with her father. The distinction between what is familiar and what is strange begins to become less clear; she feels a new distance between herself and her family home: 'I loved it because I knew it, but I was aware now of its dullness' (p.51).

Finding her place in the household (pp.51–7)

- Develops theme of transition.
- Descriptions/analyses of Tanneke, Catharina, Maria Thins and the children.
- Importance of the studio.

Griet gradually settles into the routines of her new life. She begins to 'find [her] place at the house on Oude Langendijck' (p.51), and learns ways to avoid conflict with Tanneke and Catharina. Catharina's pregnancy makes her 'ungainly' (p.52) and Maria Thins begins unlocking the studio door for Griet. Griet and Tanneke 'do more and more of her work – looking after the girls, buying things for the house, changing the baby' (p.52). Griet learns that, because Vermeer paints so slowly, the household is not as wealthy as she thought. She grows to like Maertge, Lisbeth and Aleydis, but remains 'wary of Cornelia' (p.55).

Griet increasingly feels more at home with the Vermeers than with her own family: 'Sometimes when I visited my family at home I felt awkward telling them anything. My new life was taking over the old' (p.56). One morning Maertge accompanies Griet to the fish market. She sees Agnes, but does not speak to her: 'I have two families now, and they must not mix. I was always ashamed afterwards that I had turned my back on my own sister' (p.57).

Camera obscura (pp.57–64)

- Vermeer and Griet's second conversation: what it means to 'see'.

One of the roles Vermeer plays for Griet is that of teacher. He tells her that the wooden box he has borrowed from van Leeuwenhoek is a 'camera obscura' and invites her to look in it.

Q Read pp.60–1 closely: what other roles does Vermeer play for Griet? Why is she so unsettled by his presence in the studio, and by being covered by his robe?

Griet is thrown off balance by what she sees when she first looks in the box: 'I swallowed. I was terribly confused, and a little frightened. What was in the box was a trick of the devil, or something Catholic I did not understand' (p.61). Vermeer invites her to look again. She accepts, but asks to be left alone in the studio. This time, Griet is entranced by the projected 'image' and finds it 'hard to stop looking into the box' (p.63). Note that she uses the word that Vermeer has just taught her – 'image' –

to describe what she sees. This is a story about the processes of learning, about the struggle to understand new and unfamiliar concepts. Vermeer challenges Griet to think about the complexities of what it means to 'see':

> "But why do you look at it, sir, when you can look at your own painting?"
>
> "You do not understand." He tapped the box. "This is a tool. I use it to help me see, so that I am able to make the painting."
>
> "But – you use your eyes to see."
>
> "True, but my eyes do not always see everything." (p.63)

Throughout this scene (and elsewhere in the novel) Griet is sensitive to Vermeer's authority over her: 'he was my master. I was meant to do as he said' (p.60).

The plague; Pieter's 'expectation' (pp.64–71)

- Griet an outsider.
- Compares/contrasts Vermeer and Pieter the son.

Pieter the son tells Griet that her family is likely to be quarantined because of the plague. Catharina and Maria Thins refuse her request to go to them (p.67). The next morning Vermeer tells her that the quarantine has been set. They discuss the changes he has made to the painting: '"It is a better painting now." I did not think I would have dared to say such a thing at another time, but the danger to my family had made me reckless. His smile made me grip my broom tightly' (p.68).

Q Griet feels 'unsettled' (p.65) for a number of reasons at this point in the novel. What are they?

Griet is distracted from work by her fear for her family. The quarantine means that on Sunday she can neither go home nor go to her family's church: 'I did not want to remain at the house, though – whatever Catholics did on Sundays, I did not want to be among them' (p.68). Griet's fear for her family makes her feel her difference from the Vermeers more acutely. She attends the service at the New Church, but – surrounded by wealthy Protestants in the grand church – she feels 'like a mouse hiding in a rich man's house' (p.69).

The description of Griet's conversation with Vermeer – her gratitude for his expression of concern for her family, the 'kindness in his eyes' (p.67) – is recalled when she talks with Pieter the son a few pages later. The interest both men show in her unsettles and confuses her, but she begins to imagine Pieter in her future: 'The creases between his nails and his fingers were filled with blood. I expect I will have to get used to that sight, I thought' (p.71). Moments such as this suggest that Griet's hardest task will be to accept what her future holds, where she belongs and with whom she belongs. When he tells her that Agnes is very ill, Griet meets Pieter's gaze for the first time: 'I looked into his eyes and saw kindness there. I also saw what I had feared – expectation' (p.71).

Frans; Catharina and Vermeer; van Ruijven (pp.72–7)

- Van Ruijven's interest in Griet established; parallel between Vermeer and van Ruijven.
- Griet visits Frans to tell him about Agnes. He is clearly unhappy at the tile factory.

Vermeer finishes the painting of van Ruijven's wife. Griet delays clearing away the things he has been painting. Rather than scold her for cleaning too slowly, Vermeer helps Griet tidy the room. His behaviour suggests a sympathy between them, a shared attachment to the process of making a beautiful painting. Griet explains: 'I'm so used to the objects where they are that I hate to move them' (p.74).

Griet attracts the attention of Vermeer's patron, van Ruijven. It is significant that van Ruijven uses the same words Vermeer has used earlier to describe Griet. He calls her the 'wide-eyed maid' (pp.76 and 77).

Key point

The novel asks us to compare Vermeer's and van Ruijven's attitudes to Griet; it would be inaccurate to describe Vermeer as the book's hero and van Ruijven as its villain.

Agnes' death (pp.77–80)

Griet grieves for her sister, but Agnes' death does not bring her family closer together. Both Griet and Frans find their visits home increasingly difficult (p.80). Griet is coming to the painful realisation that her life can never return to the way it was before her father's accident.

Birth feast; Pieter, Vermeer, van Ruijven (pp.81–92)

- Close focus on relationship between Griet and principal male characters.
- Explores link between looking (and being looked at) and sexual desire.

Catharina gives birth to Franciscus. Griet watches Vermeer's reaction closely: 'It is Catharina who wants many children ... He would rather be alone in his studio' (p.82; also pp.85 and 88). Griet's attraction to her master becomes more apparent: 'I did not like to think of him in that way, with his wife and children. I preferred to think of him alone in his studio. Or not alone, but with only me' (p.82). The household prepares for the birth feast (pp.83–84). The description of the wine for the feast, 'wonderfully spiced with cinnamon' (p.85), recalls Griet's first meeting with Vermeer: 'He spoke her name as if he held cinnamon in his mouth' (p.4). This unusual simile highlights the physicality of Vermeer's relationship with Catharina; he also 'speak[s] to her in a low voice laced with honey' (p.82). The birth of Franciscus makes Griet acutely aware of the sexual relationship Vermeer has with his wife: 'I knew how babies were made. He had his part to play, and he must have played it willingly' (p.82).

Pieter delivers the meat for the birth feast to Griet. Vermeer watches them. As happens so often in this book, the focus is on the way the characters look at each other:

> I turned to look at him, and saw that he had seen Pieter's smile, and the expectation there as well.
>
> He transferred his grey eyes to me. They were cold. I felt dizzy, as if I had stood up too quickly. I turned back round. Pieter's smile was not so wide now. He had seen my dizziness.

> I felt caught between the two men. It was not a pleasant feeling. (p.86)

Key point

This tense encounter is a turning point in the narrative. It establishes Vermeer and Pieter as rivals for Griet's loyalty and affection; she feels 'caught between the two men'.

Remember that we see all of the characters through Griet's eyes; we read only her side of the story. The relationship between looking (and being looked at) and sexual desire, which is illustrated in this scene, is also an issue for Griet during the birth feast, when she again finds herself the object of competing male gazes. This time the competition is between Vermeer and van Ruijven: 'I could feel two pairs of eyes on my back' (p.88).

Q What role does Pieter's father play in this scene?

Q 'Worst of all he was angry with me' (p.89). What do you make of Griet's interpretation of Vermeer's behaviour after the feast and the scene with Pieter? Is she a reliable narrator?

'1664' concludes with Griet and Vermeer together in his studio where she provides the inspiration for him to start painting again. The artist interrupts Griet cleaning the windows and she looks over her shoulder at him: 'He was studying me. He was interested in me again' (p.91).

1665 (pp.93–180)

Summary: *Griet assists Vermeer; struggles to maintain her relationship with her family; comes to see Pieter the son as a means of escape. Van Ruijven demands a painting of her.*

Griet's father and Vermeer; Griet begins assisting Vermeer; Cornelia breaks tile (pp.95–103).

- *Young Woman with a Water Pitcher.*
- Illustrates growing ambivalence of Griet's feelings for her parents.

Griet's discussion with her father about Vermeer's latest painting and her conversation with her mother about Pieter show that she feels ambivalent towards them. She both cares deeply for her parents and is increasingly frustrated by them. She rates Vermeer's paintings more highly than her father's tiles, and is irritated by his failure to visualise the painting she describes. She sees subtlety and depth in her master's art, which she contrasts to the everyday simplicity of her father's tiles. Whereas tile painters use only different shades of blue on white, Vermeer's use of colour is more complex. Her father finds this distinction confusing. He says, 'Blue is blue':

> And a tile is a tile, I thought, and nothing like his paintings. I wanted him to understand that white was not simply white. It was a lesson my master had taught me. (p.96)

Griet's visit to her parents takes place two months after Franciscus' birth. Soon after the birth she begins 'assisting' (p.99) Vermeer. On a bitterly cold day, Catharina asks her to collect some remedies for her sick sons from the apothecary. Visiting the apothecary is usually considered a privilege because of his 'respected' (p.99) position in the community, but on this occasion being asked to run the errand indicates Griet's low status in the household (p.100). However, when Vermeer asks her to get some things for him as well, she is pleased by the request (p.100). The apothecary's response reinforces the suggestion that for Vermeer to ask his maid to collect painting materials for him somehow makes her more important: 'He's never had anyone fetch the makings of colours for him before ... He always gets them himself. This is a surprise' (pp.101–02). The apothecary also suggests that, like Catharina, he may simply have sent her to avoid the cold. Still, Griet perceives immediately that 'it was best if no one knew I had run an errand for him' (p.103). Cornelia sees Griet give Vermeer the package. She fears that Cornelia may use the information against her. Soon after this incident she discovers that her belongings have been disturbed and her favourite tile broken. She guesses that Cornelia is responsible (p.103).

Vermeer teaches Griet about painting (pp.104–11)

Griet spends more time assisting Vermeer – running errands, laying out his paints, acting as a model. She follows Vermeer's lead and continues to keep her changing role a secret. Read Griet's account of standing in for the baker's daughter closely. It is a very important moment in the text. Griet finds the experience both uncomfortable and fascinating. She blushes under the intensity of Vermeer's gaze. He tells Griet, 'Don't look at what you are looking at ... I can see it in your face. It is distracting you' (p.105). When this doesn't settle her, he asks her to close her eyes. It is the artist's job to look; the model is there to be looked at. The comparison with her blind father confirms this point: 'This must be how my father feels ... with the space all around him, and his body knowing where it is' (p.105).

Vermeer teaches Griet how to prepare the coloured powders he uses to make paints. These new tasks make it more difficult for her to hide the fact that she is assisting him, but Vermeer does nothing to make things easier for Griet. He neither aids nor deceives, nor does he seem to accept responsibility for the position in which he has placed her. Griet does ask for his help, but still he does nothing: 'I hated to question or disobey him – he was my master. But I feared the anger of the women downstairs' (p.110).

Griet moves into attic; Cornelia exposes Griet's secret (pp.111–22)

- Attraction to Vermeer intensifies.
- Confrontation with Tanneke.

At Vermeer's suggestion, Griet begins sleeping in the attic. Catharina initially disapproves, but agrees when Vermeer says that she would have to lock Griet in at night: 'Perhaps she thought locking me away would keep me both safely in one place and out of her sight' (p.113). The fact that Griet never sleeps in the main part of the house emphasises her status as an outsider in the household; she does not belong. Although Griet does not like being locked in at night, she enjoys her time in the attic and the studio, and it makes it easier for her to assist Vermeer. She begins to make excuses to go to the attic in the afternoons: 'I began to get used to lying' (p.114). Maria Thins discovers her secret. She thinks that Griet's help makes him paint faster, so aids in the deception (p.117).

Q 'So this is what you've been up to, eh, girl?' (Maria Thins, p.116) Why do Griet and the other characters act as though she, rather than Vermeer, is to blame for her deceptive behaviour? Why does Maria Thins insist on keeping Griet's new role a secret from Catharina and Tanneke?

Griet spends more time alone with Vermeer: 'I grew used to being around him' (p.115); 'When he stood close to me I could feel the warmth of his body' (p.116). Griet's attraction to her master becomes more apparent. Her fantasy about modelling for one of his paintings also suggests a fantasy about taking the place of his wife: 'I imagined wearing the yellow and black bodice and pearls, holding a glass of wine, sitting across the table from him' (p.118).

Cornelia reveals Griet's secret to Tanneke. Griet instructs her to speak to Maria Thins rather than Catharina: 'she would never forgive me for treating her as if she were below me' (p.121). Tanneke does as Griet says, but their relationship is strained as a result.

Willem Bolnes; Pieter meets Griet's family (pp.122–31)

Pieter the son tells Griet the story of Willem Bolnes.

Q Why does Pieter's story upset and confuse Griet? Why does it make her remember the 'knife spinning on my mother's kitchen floor' (p.125)?

Pieter begins to attend Sunday services at Griet's church. She is acutely aware of being seen 'with him in front of so many watchful eyes' (p.127; also p.126). Her mother encourages the relationship by asking Griet to meet him and later by inviting him to Sunday lunch. Griet does not welcome Pieter's attention, but she accepts it anyway: 'I had not played this game with a man before, but I had seen what went on with others.

If Pieter was serious, then my parents would have to treat him seriously' (p.128).

After lunch, Griet's mother tells her to walk with Pieter. Again, she is conscious of being seen with him:

> I walked beside him, sure that our neighbours were staring, though in truth it was a rainy day and there were few people out. I felt as if my parents had pushed me into the street, that a deal had been made and I was being passed into the hands of a man. At least he is a good man, I thought, even if his hands are not as clean as they could be. (p.129)

There is a deliberate comparison here between Griet's parents sending her to live as Vermeer's maid and sending her to live as Pieter's wife (see 'Themes, Ideas & Values'). The reference to Pieter's hands draws our attention to this. We know that Vermeer's hands are clean, but is he a good man? Griet lets Pieter kiss her but she remains unmoved.

Vermeer's paintings; van Leeuwenhoek; Griet changes painting (pp.131–44)

- *The Girl with the Wineglass; A Lady Writing.*
- Griet's possible future.

Vermeer completes the painting of the baker's daughter. The baker is a minor character who is used to provide a contrast to van Ruijven. Griet ranks the baker's 'honest response' (p.132) to the painting above the wealthier man's 'honeyed words and studied expressions' (p.133). Throughout the novel Griet judges other characters according to how they respond to Vermeer's paintings. This middle section of the book pays the closest attention to the paintings themselves. Van Ruijven wants a painting of his wife 'looking out' (p.134). Griet learns about the 'scandal' (p.134) that surrounded *The Girl with the Wineglass*, an earlier painting depicting two men and a girl in a red dress. Pieter tells her that the girl was van Ruijven's maid and that, after being encouraged by her master to drink too much wine while sitting for the painting, she became pregnant to him.

Q '"What happened to her?" Pieter shrugged. "What happens to girls like that?" His words froze my blood.' (p.135) Why does this story have such an impact on Griet?

Vermeer begins another painting of van Ruijven's wife.

Key point

By this stage, Griet is aware of a number of possibilities for her future. She feels the pressure of Pieter and her family's expectation, and is aware of the threat van Ruijven poses to her. She is also aware of the restrictions placed upon her by her low social and economic status. She feels trapped by her circumstances.

Vermeer sends her to fetch Catharina's fur-trimmed mantle and pearl jewellery for van Ruijven's wife to wear. Holding the 'riches', she glimpses the possibility of escape to an unknown and independent future: 'I could go to the star in the middle of Market Square, choose a direction to follow, and never come back' (p.136; also p.151). We already know enough about Griet to guess that she will never make this choice.

Griet meets van Leeuwenhoek. He is portrayed as a considerate and attentive man. He teases Vermeer: 'Next you'll be teaching her to paint your women for you' (p.139). This comment raises the possibility of a future that Griet is never allowed to seriously consider or pursue. The novel draws our attention to Griet's artistic potential in the next scene. She stands behind Vermeer as he paints van Ruijven's wife: 'I stood behind him for a moment to look at the setting with her in it' (p.140). Griet recognises the problem with the painting before Vermeer does: 'I pondered each object ... and decided what I would change' (p.141). She waits for Vermeer to alter the setting, to introduce some 'disorder' (p.141) into the scene. She finds the waiting unbearable and rearranges the blue cloth in the setting herself: 'He may send me away for changing it, but it is better now' (p.142). Griet is happy when she sees that Vermeer has painted her change: 'I lay in bed that night smiling in the dark' (p.144).

Key point

This is perhaps Griet's happiest moment. It is also the closest she ever comes to being a painter herself.

When Vermeer asks her to explain the change, she responds carefully and intelligently. He is surprised by her response: 'I had not thought I would learn something from a maid' (p.144).

Catholic paintings? (pp.145–50)

- Focuses on the question of religious difference.

According to Griet's mother, Vermeer's 'paintings are not good for the soul' (p.145). It is not clear whether she disapproves more of Vermeer's paintings, or of her daughter's response to them: 'There is something dangerous about your description of his paintings ... You give the painting meaning that it does not have or deserve' (p.145). She insists that paintings are everyday objects, seen by everyone and readily available.

> "Working for them has turned your head ... It's made you forget who you are and where you come from. We're a decent Protestant family whose needs are not ruled by riches or fashions." (p.146)

Griet asks Vermeer, 'Are your paintings Catholic paintings?' (p.147). He tells her, 'It's not the painting that is Catholic or Protestant ... but the people who look at it, and what they expect to see' (p.148).

Q To what extent does Griet's religious upbringing determine how she responds to Vermeer's paintings? What other factors influence her?

Jewellery box; Griet's grandmother's comb (pp.150–61)

- Griet begins to accept Pieter; Catharina pregnant again.
- Themes: impact of stereotypes on our perceptions and treatment of others; difficulty of finding a place to belong.

The idea that people see what they expect to see is explored further in the story of Catharina and Griet's combs. Just as Griet's mother's attitude to Vermeer's paintings is based on her assumptions about Catholics, so too Catharina's distrust of Griet is based on the stereotype of a maid: 'Stealing and tempting the master of the house – that was what mistresses were always looking for in maids' (p.150). Maertge tells Griet that Catharina is unhappy about her jewellery box being in the studio with Griet: 'She said either you or the jewellery box must go' (p.151). Griet is distressed by the thought of continuing to work in Vermeer's house as an ordinary maid, without the 'chance of beauty or colour or light in my life' (p.151). She realises that Pieter the son represents the possibility of 'escape' (p.153).

Cornelia frames Griet for the theft of Catharina's ivory comb. Griet asks Vermeer for help and Cornelia is punished. Maria Thins tells Griet, 'he has backed you, in his way ... and that is more powerful than anything Catharina or Cornelia or Tanneke or even I may say against you' (p.157). Rather than speaking in Griet's defence, Maria Thins tells her that Vermeer 'charged [Catharina] with failing to raise her children properly. Much cleverer, you see, to criticise her than to praise you' (p.157). He did not tell his wife that Griet assists him, but Maria Thins did: 'It's nonsense, you sneaking around, keeping secrets from her in her own house' (p.157). After this, Griet notices changes in the way the other women treat her.

Q Why does Cornelia switch the combs? What does her grandmother's comb symbolise for Griet?

Q How does the behaviour of the other women in the household change towards Griet? Is her position more or less stable after this episode?

Q Griet is 'disappointed' (p.161) in Vermeer. Does she expect too much?

Van Ruijven wants a painting of Griet (pp.161–71)

- Griet's vulnerability to powerful men.

Vermeer finishes *A Lady Writing*. The van Ruijvens and van Leeuwenhoek attend a 'special dinner' (p.162) at the house. Maria Thins arranges for Griet to help serve the meal. Van Ruijven behaves as expected: 'he managed to slide his hand along my thigh' (p.163). Again, Griet is intensely aware of being watched by men: 'Van Ruijven's eyes followed me everywhere. So did my master's'; 'van Leeuwenhoek noted everything' (p.163). Van Ruijven announces that he wants to be in a painting with Griet.

Q Why does Maria Thins put Griet in such an awkward (and dangerous) position? How do the other characters react?

Q What do we learn about van Leeuwenhoek in this scene?

Griet's mother and the butchers have heard gossip that Vermeer is to paint her. Griet talks to Maria Thins: 'I do not wish to sit with van Ruijven, madam. I do not think his intentions are honourable' (p.167). She replies that Vermeer does not want to paint her with Ruijven, but adds that they 'cannot afford to offend him' (p.167). Griet seeks out Pieter the son and assures him that the rumours are false. Their conversation is an important one. Pieter believes her, but warns her of the vulnerability of her position: 'But you have little power over what happens to you. Surely you can see that?' (p.169). He offers her a future in which she would not be so 'helpless', in which she would not 'become like the maid in the red dress': 'We would run our own business, earn our own money, rule our own lives. Isn't that what you want?' (pp.169–70).

Q 'I was a fool even to hesitate' (p.170). Why does Griet refuse to answer Pieter's question?

***The Concert*; Frans; *The Procuress* (pp.171–80)**

- Themes: growing up; relationships between men and women.

Vermeer begins *The Concert*. Maria Thins sends Griet on errands to keep her away from van Ruijven. He sits for the painting with his sister and daughter. Griet visits her parents and her brother. She finds Frans working in the kiln room at the tile factory. He has not advanced to painting tiles like the other apprentices. She learns that this is his punishment for showing interest in the owner's wife: 'She showed her interest, you see. But when I showed mine she told her husband' (p.176). When Griet tells

Frans about van Ruijven, his response silences her: 'It's clear from your face. You want [your master]' (p.177).

Q 'Frans! How could you be so stupid? You know she's not for the likes of you. To endanger your place for something like that!' (p.176) Does Griet judge her brother too harshly? Is his situation all that different from her own?

Vermeer asks Griet to come to the studio. She studies the setting for his new painting. He asks Griet to sit facing the window and look back over her shoulder towards him: 'My eyes filled with tears I did not shed. I knew now ... He was going to paint me' (p.180).

Q Read the description of Dirck van Baburen's painting, *The Procuress* (p.179; also p.193). How is Griet like the young woman in the painting? Who do the man and old woman in the painting represent?

1666 (pp.181–229)

Summary: *Griet moves further away from her family; feels caught between Pieter the son and Vermeer; continues to resist van Ruijven; is painted by Vermeer; leaves Maria Thins' house.*

Griet's family; lies and secrets (pp.183–6)

- Symbolic importance of Griet's cap.

Key point

Each year begins with a scene in Griet's parents' house. Chevalier uses these scenes to illustrate the changes in Griet's attitudes to her family.

Q 'You smell of linseed oil.' Read p.183. How has Griet's relationship with her father changed?

Griet becomes more involved with the butcher. She lets him do more to her in the alley, but she only responds to his touch when she thinks of Vermeer (p.185). On this day, he surprises her by running his hands up under her cap and touching her hair: 'Some day soon, Griet, I will see all of this. You will not always be a secret to me' (p.186).

Q Why does Griet keep her hair covered? (See also pp.130–1.)

Q Pieter tells Griet, '"... your family needs me" ... I did not like being reminded of his power over us' (p.186). Look again at Pieter and Griet's conversation (p.169). How is Pieter's power the same as / different from van Ruijven and Vermeer's? Is Griet also 'helpless' (p.169) in her relationship with him?

Vermeer decides how to paint Griet (pp.187–94)

- The entanglement of history and fiction.

This scene a very important stage in the narrative. It makes it clear that much of what has happened in the novel so far has been about the painting of Griet. The difficulty Vermeer has deciding how to paint Griet playfully draws our attention to the entanglement of fact and fiction that makes this book so fascinating. The artist tries various poses and props: 'All the while he seemed perplexed, as if someone had told him a story and he couldn't recall the ending' (p.189).

Key point

The 'ending' of the story has already been written in the 'real' world. Historical fact places limits on Chevalier and her characters. Vermeer can only paint Griet one way: wearing a blue and yellow turban, looking over her shoulder towards the artist, her face bathed in light. Chevalier's creativity comes into play when she imagines the meaning of each of these elements.

Q Vermeer allows Griet a say in how he paints her. How does she want to be painted? What do you think her reasons are?

Vermeer and van Ruijven (pp.195–201)

- Theme: relationships between men and women.
- Similarity between Griet and Catharina.

Van Leeuwenhoek warns Griet about Vermeer: 'He is interested in you in part because van Ruijven is' (p.197). He tells her to hold on to who she is: 'The women in his paintings – he traps them in his world. You can get lost there' (p.197). The description of Catharina that follows this conversation suggests a similarity between the two women. They are both, in a sense, 'trapped' by their ties to Vermeer: Catharina by an apparently unhappy marriage and family life; Griet by the intensity of her feelings for him. He has a hold on both of their bodies. (A few pages earlier, when Griet first poses for the painting, she feels 'a ripple of heat [pass] through [her] body', p.191.) The threat van Ruijven poses to Griet is more explicit. He begins to seek her out when he visits the house: 'I pushed him away as politely as a maid can a gentleman. None the less he managed to become familiar with the shape of my breasts and thighs under my clothes' (p.199).

Catharina's pearl (pp.201–15)

- Griet's artistic potential.
- Symbolic significance of Griet's hair.
- Frans' escape.

Again, Griet sees what is wrong with Vermeer's painting before he does, but this time she does not try to help him: 'When I saw what was needed – that point of brightness he had used to catch the eye in other paintings – I shivered. This will be the end, I thought' (p.203). She does not want to wear Catharina's pearls. When Griet sees Vermeer looking at the earring ('On his face was his painter's look'), she spills wine on Catharina's belly ('A few drops of red had splashed there') (p.204). The image recalls the red powder Cornelia smeared on Griet's apron and foreshadows the role Cornelia's mischief will play in Griet's future, the death of the child Catharina is carrying, and Griet's future life as a butcher's wife.

Vermeer surprises Griet preparing her headdress in the attic:

> Now that he had seen my hair, now that he had seen me revealed, I no longer felt I had something precious to hide and keep to myself. I could be freer, if not with him, then with someone else. It no longer mattered what I did and did not do. (p.208)

This passage clarifies the symbolic link between Griet's hair and her sexuality. She sneaks from the house that evening to find Pieter: 'I pulled up my skirt and let him do as he liked' (p.208). The next time she sits for Vermeer he asks her to open her mouth: 'Virtuous women did not open their mouths in paintings. It was as if he had been in the alley with Pieter and me' (p.210). He insists Griet must wear the earring.

Griet plans to ask Frans to pierce her ear, but the woman at the tile factory tells her he has gone. Griet notices that the woman is pregnant. She buys clove oil to numb her earlobe and pierces it herself. The first few months of 1666 are very difficult for Griet. She has come to realise the wisdom of van Leeuwenhoek's warning to her ('He used what he wanted for his paintings, without considering the result', p.207); the loss of her brother makes her feel 'more alone than ever' (p.211); and van Ruijven continues to harass her.

Griet's eighteenth birthday; Pieter and Vermeer; Vermeer completes painting (pp.215–23)

- Griet and Vermeer – the pearl earrings.

On the morning of Griet's eighteenth birthday, Maria Thins hands Griet the pearl earrings and sends her to the studio for her final sitting with Vermeer. When she has changed into her headdress, Griet looks again at *The Procuress* (p.218). The relevance of this painting becomes clearer when Tanneke calls Griet a 'whore' (p.220) after she refuses Pieter's marriage proposal.

Vermeer finishes the painting. He pushes the earring through the hole in her ear: 'He traced the side of my face up to my cheek, then blotted the tears that spilled from my eyes with his thumb. He ran his thumb over my lower lip. I licked it and tasted salt' (p.221). He insists that she pierce her other ear as well. When the painting is finished, Griet feels discarded, used. She waits for him to come to her in the storeroom, her 'hair out over [her] shoulders, but he did not come. Now that the painting was finished he no longer wanted me' (p.222).

Q What do you think Griet means here?

Catharina sees painting; Griet leaves (pp.223–9)

Cornelia shows her mother the painting. Catharina is outraged and sends for her husband. While Griet waits to see what will happen to her, she notices the warmth of the day: 'Tomorrow might be bitterly cold, but today it was spring' (p.225). This is a hopeful moment in the text; spring is a time of new beginnings. Griet blames Cornelia: 'I wanted to slap her as I had that first day' (p.225). Neither Maria Thins nor Vermeer come to Griet's defence when Catharina accuses her of stealing the earrings (p.226). This is a beautifully written section of the novel. Griet imagines what she might have said, but says very little, and the other characters barely speak to her. She watches the action as though from a distance, looking at the other characters carefully and interpreting their behaviour. She sees that Catharina knows the earrings are not the 'real matter' (p.227).

The scene in Vermeer's studio is one of the most powerful episodes in the novel. Catharina behaves 'wildly' (p.228). She grabs Vermeer's painting knife and tries to damage the painting of Griet. Vermeer stops her 'just before the blade touched my eye' (p.228). The narrative returns to where it began with the image of the knife spinning across the floor towards Griet: 'It came to a stop with the blade pointed at me' (p.228). In the opening scene of the novel, Griet picks up the knife from the floor of her mother's kitchen and wipes it on her apron: 'That was what maids were meant to do – pick up their master's and mistress' things and put them back in their place' (p.228). This time, however, she does not pick up the knife, but simply turns and leaves the room. She runs to the eight-pointed star in the centre of Delft: 'Each point indicated a direction I could take' (p.229).

Q Chevalier uses the image of a spinning knife to great effect. What do you think it means? Why does Catharina aim the blade at the picture of Griet's eye? Why does the knife point towards Griet when it stops spinning? Why doesn't she pick it up?

1676 (pp. 231–48)

Summary: *Vermeer has died. Griet is married to Pieter and has two sons. She returns to Maria Thins' house for the first time in ten years. According to Vermeer's wishes, Catharina gives Griet the pearl earrings. She sells them and decides to keep the truth from Pieter.*

- Functions as an epilogue to the main action.
- Themes: secrecy and lies; choice.

Early in the epilogue there are references to Griet's butcher's knife: 'When I looked up and saw [Tanneke] I almost dropped my knife' (p.233). These provide an important link to the main narrative (also p.239). We learn that Griet and Pieter were married soon after the 'day of the painting and the palette knife' (p.235) and that she has never told him about everything that happened to her. They have two children: Jan and Frans. The narrator of the epilogue is an older, wiser Griet, than the narrator of the main narrative. She says, 'For a long time I thought I might still matter to him. After a while, though, I admitted to myself that he had always cared more for the painting of me than for me' (p.237).

Griet returns to the Oude Langendijck. Some of Vermeer's children are sitting together on the bench outside the house. Franciscus recognises her from the painting. He tells her that Vermeer borrowed it from van Ruijven before his death. She meets with Catharina and van Leeuwenhoek, who is acting as the executor of Vermeer's will. Catharina explains the circumstances surrounding her husband's death: his 'frenzy' (p.245) as a result of mounting debt. Her clothing betrays the family's fall in circumstance. She has trouble concealing her hostility towards Griet when she fulfils Vermeer's wish and gives her the pearl earrings (p.246). Cornelia taunts Griet as she is leaving the house: 'You could give them to me' (p.247). Griet slaps her.

Griet sells the earrings for twenty guilders and decides to lie to Pieter. She will tell him that the Vermeers repaid their debt of fifteen guilders and hide the remainder: 'Pieter would be pleased ... the debt now settled. I would not have cost him anything. A maid came free' (p.248).

CHARACTERS & RELATIONSHIPS

- Try drawing a character map.
- Develop your own point of view about all of the characters and their relationships. Find evidence in the text to support your arguments. The questions included here are designed to help with this.

Griet

Key quotes

'Strangers would think I was calm. I did not cry as a baby. Only my mother would note the tightness along my jaw, the widening of my already wide eyes.' (p.3) For other references to Griet's 'wide eyes' see pp.62, 77, 162 and 178.

'I could not say why I had laid out the vegetables as I did. I simply set them as I felt they should be, but I was too frightened to say so to a gentleman.' (Vermeer, p.5)

'This was how I cleaned without seeming to move anything. I measured each thing in relation to the objects around it and the space between them. The small things on the table were easy, the furniture harder – I used my feet, my knees, sometimes my shoulders and chin with the chairs.' (p.36)

'Ah, you're a cunning one, girl. You know whose pot to spoon from. Never mind, we can do with a bit of cleverness around here.' (Maria Thins, p.48)

Griet's point of view

Griet is both the central character of *Girl with a Pearl Earring* and the novel's narrator (See 'Genre, Style & Structure'). Remember that we see all of the other characters from Griet's point of view. It is important that you keep this point in mind as you are forming your opinions about the other characters and their relationships to Griet and to each other.

Q Is Griet a good judge of character? Consider particularly the first descriptions of Tanneke (p.16), Cornelia (p.15), Vermeer and Catharina (pp.2–3) in the context of the rest of the novel.

Griet's visual perception

The story of Griet's transition from childhood to adulthood forms the main narrative. From the opening scene we are made aware of Griet's emotional and visual sensitivity to her surroundings. The circle of colour she makes out of chopped vegetables in this scene is used throughout the novel to symbolise her artistic sensibility. It signals also the special link between Griet and Vermeer. Initially employed to clean his studio and work as a maid in his household, she later becomes his assistant, and finally his model. Not only does she prepare Vermeer's colours for him, but Greit and the artist both see the world through 'painter's eyes' (p.9). Both Griet and Vermeer value composition, colour, the play of light on objects, and the relationship between these things. One of the saddest aspects of this novel is that while Griet shares her master's heightened aesthetic sense, she can never be an artist herself. Her gender, her youth, and her low economic and social status mean that she must play less important and less powerful roles: maid, assistant, model.

Griet's status as an outsider

The experience of living with and working for the Vermeers forces Griet to face the question of her difference from others, and to confront the issue of belonging. She feels like an outsider from the moment she leaves the Market Square and crosses into Papist's Corner. Eventually, however, living in Vermeer's household makes Griet feel as though she doesn't belong anywhere (p.56).

Q Is there anywhere Griet feels she truly belongs?

Q How is she the same as / different from other characters?

Chevalier says that making Griet 'an outsider' was a deliberate choice:

> I thought that an outsider has an ability to look at something afresh and stirs up stuff. What could have been quite a static household ends up not being static because of her arrival. At the beginning, her family's house was all she knew, that was the base she came from. After she had the experience of

> living with the Vermeers for a while, going back home was hard. It's a combination of being an outsider and also being 16 – it's not like anyone talked about adolescent rebellion back then, but there probably would have been that feeling that something was going to change, and she was going to feel alienated from her family. (quoted in Grant 2001)

Just as meeting Vermeer initiates a process of change and self-development for Griet, so too she is the catalyst for change in the artist's household. When she returns ten years later, Maria Thins recalls her impact on the household: 'The most trouble we've ever had with a maid' (p.242). Think also about Griet's status as the only 'fictional' character living in the house. Chevalier describes the novel's setting as a 'static household' into which she introduces a fictional element to stir things up. Griet is an outsider in several senses.

- The analyses of other characters below focus on their relationships with Griet. Also see 'Themes, Ideas & Values'.

Q Tracy Chevalier has said: 'I've always loved the painting ... It's seemingly simple. It is just a girl looking at you. But I feel like she mirrors my mood. When I am sad she looks sad, when I am happy she looks happy. I wanted to explain that look on her face' (quoted in Schumacher 2000). Do you think she achieved her goal? How might Chevalier have imagined the girl's life differently?

Johannes Vermeer

Key quotes

'The man was watching me, his eyes grey like the sea. He had a long, angular face, and his expression was steady, in contrast to his wife's, which flickered like a candle. He had no beard or moustache, and I was glad, for it gave him a clean appearance. He wore a black cloak over his shoulders, a white shirt, and a fine lace collar. His hat pressed into hair the red of brick washed by rain.' (pp.4–5)

'Hearing his voice made me feel as if I were walking along the edge of a canal and unsure of my steps. I did not know how he would treat me in his own house, whether or not he would pay attention to the vegetables I chopped in his kitchen. No gentleman had ever taken such an interest in me before.' (p.44)

'He saw things in a way that others did not, so that a city I had lived in all my life seemed a different place, so that a woman became beautiful with the light on her face.' (p. 64)

'I felt alone there, perched high above the noisy household, able to see it from a distance. Rather like him.' (p.117)

Fact/fiction

Chevalier imagines Vermeer with eyes 'grey ... like the inside of an oyster shell' (p.180), and 'hair the red of brick washed by rain' (p.5). However, as she says on the novel's website, 'we don't know what Vermeer looked like. There are no confirmed images of him'. She based her physical descriptions on men depicted in two of his paintings. In *The Procuress,* a red-haired man at the edge of the scene looks out at us. Such a figure often represented a self-portrait in paintings of the period. In *The Art of Painting,* an artist sits with his back to the viewer. There is no evidence that this is a painting of Vermeer, but Chevalier says 'it gives us some idea of what an artist in his studio may have looked like'.

Q Find a copy of *The Procuress* and *The Art of Painting* and compare them with Chevalier's descriptions of Vermeer.

Q Susan Vreeland, author of the Vermeer-inspired novel *Girl in Hyacinth Blue,* says, 'I think Vermeer provides a moment of calm and tranquillity in an age that moves too fast ... He gives us permission ... to be still a moment' (quoted in Schumacher 2000). Chevalier turned to Vermeer's paintings to help her imagine what he looked like. How did the paintings influence her idea of his personality?

Vermeer's studio

Griet likes Vermeer's studio; it allows her to escape from the bustle of the household. It performs a similar function for Vermeer:

> It was an orderly room, empty of the clutter of everyday life. It felt different from the rest of the house, almost as if it were in another house altogether. When the door was closed it would be difficult to hear the shouts of the children, the jangle of Catharina's keys, the sweeping of our brooms. (p.35)

Descriptions of the studio provide some insight into Vermeer's personality as Chevalier imagined it. Chevalier uses the scenes in the studio and in the storage room above it to show the similarities between Vermeer and Griet: they are both outsiders; they both seek order and calm; they share a heightened degree of aesthetic perception; they both watch and describe the world around them (Griet as the novel's narrator, Vermeer as an artist) in loving detail, but from a distance.

Note, for instance, the change of pace when Griet is in the studio. The novel slows down or takes pause in these scenes: to reflect the way Griet feels in the room; to emphasise the distinction between the studio and the rest of the house; to capture the 'stillness' that art critics value in Vermeer's paintings; to develop the idea that this room nurtures and feeds Griet's capacity for aesthetic perception and appreciation. In this room, she learns how to look carefully at things, to allow her gaze to linger:

> I began to notice small things – the brushes rearranged on top of the cupboard, one of the cupboard's drawers left ajar, the palette knife balanced on the easel's ledge, a chair moved a little from its place by the door. (p.55)

Griet's teacher

One of Vermeer's key roles is that of Griet's teacher: 'I thought that you painted what you saw, using the colours you saw. He taught me' (p.106). He shows her that the relationship between things and the images that represent them is more complex than she thought. In a crucial scene, he reminds her of her circle of vegetables to teach her that clouds are never simply 'white': 'I felt as if I saw them for the first time at that moment' (p.108). He shows her also the tendency of language to simplify the world; to say that clouds are 'white', or that a woman's dress is 'blue', only tells part of the story. 'After that I could not stop looking at things.' (p.108)

Q Vermeer holds a position of power relative to Griet: master/maid; man/girl (woman); teacher/student; artist/model. Does he do this throughout the novel, or do their roles change?

Q Why is Griet attracted to Vermeer? Trace the main stages of their relationship.

Q Does Vermeer exploit Griet? Does she think so?

Catharina Vermeer

Key quotes

'The woman looked as if she had been blown about by the wind, although it was a calm day. Her cap was askew so that tiny blonde curls escaped and hung about her forehead like bees which she swatted at impatiently several times. Her collar needed straightening and was not as crisp as it could be ... The woman's face was like an oval serving plate, flashing at times, dull at others. Her eyes were two light brown buttons, a colour I had rarely seen coupled with blond hair. She made a show of watching me hard, but could not fix her attention on me, her eyes darting about the room.' (pp.3–4; also p.25)

'It had been clear from the moment she'd seen me chopping vegetables in my mother's kitchen that she disliked me. Her mood was not improved by the baby she carried, which made her ungainly and nothing like the graceful lady of the house she felt herself to be ... As she grew bigger she went about the house with a tired, pained look.' (p.52) For other references to Catharina's ungainly pregnant body see pp.33, 58, 76 and 198.

'Catharina remained in bed with Franciscus, tended by the nurse, serene as a swan. Like a swan too, though, she had a long neck and sharp beak.' (p.85)

> 'Although Catharina was not feeding him herself, she insisted that Franciscus sleep in a cradle next to her. I thought this a strange arrangement, but when I came to know Catharina better I understood that she wanted to hold on to the appearance of motherhood, if not the tasks themselves.' (p.111)

Catharina and Vermeer

Read closely the detailed descriptions of Catharina (pp.3–4) and Vermeer (pp.4–5) in the novel's opening scene. They tell us a great deal about these key characters and their relationship. For instance, little details about Catharina's appearance (her cap, her flyaway hair, her badly pressed collar) hint that their position of wealth and privilege may not be a stable one. Note also the emphasis on both characters' eyes (and on the way they look at Griet and at what is around them): Catharina 'made a show of watching me hard, but could not fix her attention on me, her eyes darting about the room' (p.4). Vermeer's gaze is steady. Like Griet, he watches the people and things around him with quiet concentration.

Catharina and Griet

It is clear from the opening scene that Catharina will not make Griet feel welcome. Descriptions of Catharina highlight the differences between Griet and her mistress. While Griet hides her feelings from others, Catharina's unruly appearance (p.25) and erratic behaviour reveal her lack of inner calm. She is 'annoyed' (p.6) by her husband's interest in the circle of vegetables, but directs her disapproval at Griet. Most importantly, Catharina resents Griet's access to her husband's studio, where she is not welcome herself.

Q '... she knew little more about being my mistress than I did about being her maid.' (p.25) Trace the main stages in Griet's relationship with Catharina.

Q Why does Vermeer keep it a secret from Catharina that Griet is assisting him, and later that he is painting her?

Q Why ... have you never painted me?' (p.227) Why is Catharina so distressed when she sees the painting of Griet?

Maria Thins

Key quotes

'She was the kind of old woman who looked as if she would outlive everyone … She had the manner of someone used to looking after those less able than she – of looking after Catharina.' (p.18)

"It became clear to me that in spite of her shrewd ways, Maria Thins was soft on the people closest to her. Her judgement was not as sound as it appeared.' (p.54)

'It was clear that while he painted the works, it was she who struck the deals.' (p.132)

Early in the novel, Tanneke advises Griet on how to handle Catharina: 'Take no notice of what she says … She just orders us about because she feels she has to. But we know who our real mistress is, and so does she' (pp.53–4).

Maria Thins is undoubtedly the 'real mistress' of the house. Not only does she own the house on the Oude Langendijck, she also manages all of the people who live within it.

Q What are Maria Thins' priorities? Why does she make the decisions she does?

Q Does Maria Thins treat Griet fairly?

Tanneke

Key quotes

'The woman standing in the doorway had a broad face, pockmarked from an earlier illness. Her nose was bulbous and irregular, and her thick lips were pushed together to form a small mouth. Her eyes were light blue, as if she had caught the sky in them. She wore a grey-brown dress with a white chemise, a cap tied tight around her head, and an apron that was not as clean as mine.' (p.16)

'Although Tanneke was often bad-tempered with me, I learned not to take it to heart, as she never remained so for long. She was fickle in her moods, perhaps from being caught between Catharina and Maria Thins for so many years.' (p.54)

When Griet first meets Tanneke, she tells her that she began working for Maria Thins when she was fourteen: 'Half my life I've worked here' (p.27). Tanneke says this 'triumphantly' (p.27), but Griet is not inspired by such a future for herself: 'I would not have said such a thing with pride. Her work had worn her so that she looked older than her twenty-eight years' (p.27). When Griet returns to the house at the end of the novel, she is herself twenty-eight, but her life has followed a different path: 'I probably looked much as I had the day I first set out to work as a maid' (p.239). Tanneke represents a possible future for Griet – a life spent as a servant. When Catharina demands that Vermeer choose between Griet and her jewellery box, she imagines what her future might hold. She imagines, that is, a life like Tanneke's:

> Years of hauling water, wringing out clothes, scrubbing floors, emptying chamberpots, with no chance of beauty or colour or light in my life, stretched before me like a landscape of flat land where, a long way off, the sea is visible but can never be reached. (pp.151–2)

Q 'Already she feels threatened by me ... She will bully me if I let her.' (p.17) Tanneke's behaviour towards Griet is inconsistent. Trace the changes in her attitude.

Cornelia

Key quotes

'Cornelia picked up a pebble and threw it across the road into the canal. There were long scratches up and down her arm – she must have been bothering the house cat.' (p.22)

'Of the four girls, Cornelia was ... the most unpredictable ... She could be funny and playful one moment, then turn the next, like a purring cat who bites the hand stroking it. While loyal to her sisters, she did not hesitate to make them cry by pinching them hard. I was wary of Cornelia, and could not be fond of her in the way I came to be of the others.' (pp.54–5)

Cornelia is one of the most difficult characters in the novel to understand. The young girl's malicious behaviour makes it clear that she has an active dislike of Griet. She takes pleasure in scheming against her father's maid and is responsible for a number of key crisis points in the novel. However, Griet never offers an explanation for Cornelia's behaviour. We are given no clear insights into her motivation as we are with the other characters: 'For no particular reason but a vague distrust, she did not like me' (p.154).

Q Why does Griet slap Cornelia – both in 1664 and 1676?

Q Analyse Cornelia's relationship with her parents. Who is she most like?

Griet's parents

Key quotes

'I expected [my mother] to warn me, to tell me to be a good girl, to protect our family name. Instead she said, "Don't be rude to [Pieter]. Smile at him and be pleasant."
Her words surprised me, but when I looked in her eyes and saw there the hunger for meat that a butcher's son could provide, I understood why she had set aside her pride.' (pp.98–9)

'After my father's accident we had learned to place things where he always knew to find them. It was one thing to do this for a blind man, though. Quite another for a man with a painter's eyes.' (p.9)

Griet and her Mother

Though we do not see much of Griet's mother in the novel, we learn that she is a pragmatic woman who tries to keep her family financially stable. Griet's mother does not indulge her daughter's private feelings, knowing that Griet must face the realities of life. One such reality is that Griet must get married to survive in their society.

Q How do these circumstances affect the relationship between Griet and her mother.

Griet's father and Vermeer

Griet's conversation with her father at the beginning of the novel establishes their shared interest in Vermeer's paintings and suggests a parallel between her link with the artist and her relationship with her father (p.7). This parallel is reinforced as we read on. The image of Griet's father sitting alone by the window in the attic echoes the portrayal of Vermeer alone in his studio and the image of Griet looking out the window of her attic bedroom. These three characters share an appreciation of painting. Griet's father, however, must rely on his memory and imagination to 'see' paintings in his head. While there are clearly similarities between Griet's father and Vermeer, there are also significant differences between them. While Vermeer doesn't need to paint to put food on the table, the loss of Griet's father's ability to paint forces him to send two of his children away to work. They are of a different economic and social class. Vermeer enjoys privileges to which Griet's father has never had access. As Griet's desire for her master intensifies, she begins to find fault with her father. That Griet perceives a weakness in her father, but sees strength in her master, is suggested by the physical descriptions of the two characters: her father '... felt the cold acutely' (p.95), but 'the cold [does] not seem to affect' (p.99) Vermeer.

Griet thinks of her father as a 'tradesman' (he lost his 'trade', p.7), whereas she glorifies Vermeer as an artist. The novel draws a distinction between craft and art. Related to this is the fact that her father's work belongs to the domestic realm, but Vermeer lives in a world apart from domestic life: 'He rarely showed interest in domestic affairs' (p.112). Griet looks for her father's tiles amongst those lining the walls of the Vermeers' kitchen (p.30) and studio (p.34) whereas Vermeer's paintings are displayed in the Town Hall (p.7).

Q Both Griet's father and Vermeer belong to the same craftsmen's Guild, but their work is clearly valued quite differently – both by Griet and by society in general. How is their difference of status revealed by Griet's attitudes to them?

Q Does Griet judge her father harshly?

Pieter the son

Key quotes

'... though he was taller than his father, he had the same bright blue eyes. His blond hair was long and thick with curls, framing a face that made me think of apricots. Only his bloody apron was displeasing to the eye.' (p.42; see p.28 for description of father's bloody apron)

'I did not meet his gaze. His concern made me feel as if I had just stepped off a boat and the ground was wobbling under my feet ... He was not demanding anything the way the soldier had, but I would be obliged to him.' (pp.70–1; also p.122)

Pieter's hands

Pieter the son is a key character. He acts as a 'foil' for Vermeer. This is a useful word to understand when you come to analyse the relationship between these two characters. To describe Pieter as a 'foil' is to say that his difference from Vermeer draws our attention to the artist's qualities; he acts as a point of contrast for Griet. Her preoccupation with the two men's hands is relevant here. Pieter's blood-stained hands make her aware of Vermeer's hands. They symbolise the difference between the two men. Pieter's hands signify his class status – he is a meat worker. This idea is supported by the descriptions of Griet's hands. Her father notices that they bear 'the scars of hard work' (p.48). Her father's hands also show the evidence of work, 'his fingers still stained blue from painting ... white tiles' (p.7) in the factory. Vermeer's show no such 'scars' or 'stains': 'His hands were very clean' (p.74). He is of a higher class than Griet, Pieter and her family. His 'art' sets him apart from – and above – the workers in the novel. Pieter does not hold her attention like Vermeer does: 'When I should be listening to Pieter I found myself thinking about my master' (p.127). In a sense her master belongs to the world of fantasy for Griet (an impossible future), while Pieter the son waits for her in the 'real' world. She comes to see Pieter as a 'good man' (p.185), but is 'disappointed' (p.161) in Vermeer. Marrying Pieter represents 'escape' (p.153) from the mess that follows her involvement with her master.

Q Do you think Pieter is a 'good man' (p.185)?

Q Does Griet have any choice about marrying Pieter?

Other characters

Make your own notes about the other important characters in the novel. Find several useful quotes and identify the key elements for each character not listed above. This will help you to develop a more sophisticated and multi-layered analysis of the book. Examine the stories of Griet's siblings, Frans and Agnes. Look at the roles adult male characters play in the novel: van Ruijven, van Leeuwenhoek, Pieter, the father, and the baker. Focus in particular on the characterisation of Vermeer's patron, van Ruijven. Van Leeuwenhoek appears only briefly in the novel, but he plays an important role (see pp.138, 163 and 197). You should also pay attention to the role played by the unnamed characters in the novel. They provide a point of comparison to the central characters and reveal clues about the meaning of the main narrative. For example, Griet's experiences with the boatman and the soldier have an impact on the way she responds to Vermeer and Pieter. Consider also Griet's attitude to the market gossips and her parents' neighbours (see p.173).

Q 'Stuck in this factory day after day, nothing but white tiles as far as I can see, I think I may go mad.' (p.73) How is Frans' experience of leaving home the same as / different from Griet's?

Q 'I have two families now, and they must not mix. I was always ashamed afterwards that I had turned my back on my own sister.' (p.57) Does Griet treat her sister badly? What effect does Agnes' death have on her?

Q 'She must have learned by now what he wanted from a model. Perhaps she simply was what he wanted.' (p.137) What role does van Ruijven's wife play in the novel?

General questions

Q Make a list of the male characters in the novel. What roles do they play in relation to Griet? Try to think as creatively as you can about this question.

Q What is the hierarchy in Vermeer's household? Write a list of everyone's names, with the most powerful person at the top and the least powerful person at the bottom. Are there a number of possibilities? Try writing lists from the perspectives of key characters, e.g. Catharina, Vermeer, Tanneke.

THEMES, IDEAS & VALUES

Girl with a Pearl Earring explores a number of interlocking themes. Identifying a text's themes – and the links between them – is one of the challenges (and pleasures) of studying literature. The aim of this chapter is to answer the apparently simple question: what is the novel about? Studying this novel, and writing essays about it, will give you the opportunity to think through some fascinating and important issues. Aim to develop your own 'angle' on the book: what do you think its key theme/s is/are?

Growing up

Girl with a Pearl Earring examines one of the most fascinating and difficult stages of any individual's life: the transition from childhood to adulthood. The night before Griet first leaves home, she remembers the last time she saw her brother. She visited Frans at the tile factory and found him exhausted and disappointed: '"Father never told me it would be this bad ... He always said his apprenticeship was the making of him." "Perhaps it was," I replied. "It made him what he is now"' (p.10). In a number of senses, Griet's 'apprenticeship' to Vermeer 'makes' her into the woman she becomes. On the day it concludes, her eighteenth birthday, she 'runs' (p.229) to the eight-pointed star in the centre of town and decides which path her life will take.

Q 'Only thieves and children run.' (p.229) Why do you think Griet runs? Is Griet ready to make such a momentous decision or is she forced to make it by circumstance?

Key point

Girl with a Pearl Earring is a coming-of-age story – a bildungsroman (see 'Genre, Structure & Style'). It narrates Griet's movement from the innocence of childhood into adulthood, away from the familiarity and comfort of belonging in her parents' home and towards the newness and uncertainty of finding her own place in the world, choosing her path.

Q Griet moves away from the innocence of childhood. Does her story suggest that growing up means a loss of innocence? If so, how?

When Griet introduces Pieter the son to her parents she reassures her father that he is not losing her. His response brings tears to her eyes: 'We've already lost you … We lost you the moment you became a maid' (p.126). Griet does not welcome this period of change in her life. It brings with it the sadness of loss – of her closeness with her siblings, of the belief that her mother understands her (p.3), of her tight bond with her father.

Q What else does Griet lose during this period of her life? What does she gain?

One of the most powerful symbols of Griet's reluctance to grow up – and also of her inability to do otherwise – is the tile her father gives her on the morning she first leaves home. Read its description (p.11). Her father intends his gift to remind her of home, of the past, but if you read this passage closely, you will see that the painting on the tile is about Griet's future. It foreshadows key events: the boy walks away from his sister; he is 'mischievous'; Agnes is not in the painting; the girl on the tile wears an unusual cap. The children are 'not playing as children usually did in tiles' (p.11): this tile represents the end of their childhood. Now that their father can no longer paint tiles, they must work instead of play. *Girl with a Pearl Earring* represents growing up as a period of painful transition. As Griet walks away from her home, she realises that Agnes will have to take over her household chores: 'She would have less time to play in the street and along the canals. Her life was changing too' (p.11).

Q Compare the tile painting of Griet with Vermeer's painting of her. The girl on the tile looks away from the painter, but she looks towards him in Vermeer's painting. What do you think this means? What are the other similarities/differences between the paintings?

Note also the reference to a 'broken tile' on the following page (p.12). The image of the children throwing a broken tile into the canal takes on a special significance when you think about what happens later in the novel. This is a very well-crafted novel, which uses this kind of symbolism to tell a subtle and multi-layered tale about one girl's struggle to become a woman.

Q 'I would have been less upset if she had broken our heads from our bodies.' (p.103) Why is Griet so distressed when Cornelia breaks the tile? Why doesn't she tell her parents?

Facing the future / choices

Girl with a Pearl Earring explores the idea that our lives follow predictable patterns. It narrates Griet's realisation that the different paths her life might have followed have already been laid down for her – not just by her parents, but by the rules and conventions of the society she lives in, and by the limits her lack of wealth and status place on her. She feels the pressure of 'expectation' – from Pieter, her family and society in general – that she will behave in ways appropriate to a poor unmarried girl. Her contact with Vermeer and his paintings inspires her to imagine the possibility of a different life from the one she is destined to have: 'I wanted to wear the mantle and the pearls. I wanted to know the man who painted her like that' (p.38; also p.118).

Q Of course, Griet does eventually wear pearls, but does the experience fulfil her desires?

The eight-pointed star in the centre of Delft symbolises the fantasy of a different life for Griet – one outside the boundaries of what she knows and expects. It represents the possibility of choice. As it turns out, Griet does follow the most obvious path: she stays in Delft, marries Pieter, has children with him and works in the Meat Hall.

Early in the novel, Griet recalls a childhood game:

> ... we used to sit beside that canal and throw things in – pebbles, sticks, once a broken tile – and imagine what they might touch on the bottom – not fish, but creatures from our imagination, with many eyes, scales, hands and fins. Frans thought up the most interesting monsters. Agnes was the most frightened. I always stopped the game, too inclined to see things as they were to be able to think up things that were not. (p.12)

This passage helps to explain why Griet accepts the future which is planned for her, but Frans runs away from his apprenticeship and refuses to become a tile painter like his father. As the game by the canal illustrates, Frans is willing to imagine other worlds and possibilities, however 'monstrous' they might turn out to be. By contrast, Griet is too focused on the world close to her to imagine another one. There is, however, another explanation for their different choices. Remember that Griet is a girl. As the events in the novel make clear, this means she is more vulnerable, less powerful than her brother in the society in which she lives. Males and females are portrayed as unequal, girls have less say in what happens to them. This point is supported by the fact that whereas Griet risks ruin (being labelled a 'whore') by showing interest in her master, Frans leaves his master's wife pregnant with an illegitimate child. Despite her higher social and economic status, the master's wife, not Frans, carries the burden of their encounter.

Q How else could you interpret the novel's ending? Why do you think Griet makes a different decision from Frans?

The novel suggests that the choices we make when we're young determine our future lives. It dramatises the idea that these choices are limited by our historical context, gender and class. It provides a number of powerful metaphors for this: the spinning knife on the kitchen floor, the eight-pointed star in the centre of town. Look for other metaphors in the text that support this idea (e.g. the description of the New Church as a 'stone birdcage', p.13).

Q How limited are Griet's choices? Does the novel allow for the possibility that a girl in her position might have behaved differently (followed a different point on the star) or was her choice inevitable?

Q Griet's story is set over 300 years ago. Are the issues it explores relevant to young people today? If so, in what ways?

Difference

By writing from the perspective of an outsider, Chevalier is able to explain and investigate the complex and challenging notion of difference. The novel explores several types of difference: class, religion and gender. It shows the impact such categories have on an individual's sense of self: their understanding of who they are and where they belong.

Key point

The novel demonstrates that you come to terms with who you are by first recognising who you are not – and who you cannot be.

Q '[Tanneke] moved back into the shadowy interior so that the doorway was clear. I stepped across the threshold.' (p.17) Read Griet's description of her arrival at the Vermeer's house – it tells us much more than simply what the house looks like and who lives in it. Underline the words/phrases that suggest that Griet's difference will make it difficult for her to ever feel at home in the 'grand' (p.16) house.

Working as a maid for the Vermeers makes Griet painfully aware of her family's low social and economic status: their lack of possessions, their poor diet, their illiteracy and ignorance, their vulnerability to those more wealthy and more powerful than themselves. Maria Thins' and the Vermeers' Catholicism makes her feel alone and confused even before she first arrives at the house. Living with Catholics forces her to confront what it means to be a Protestant. She learns too about the difference between men and women (see below). These categories of difference are used to identify which groups in society have more power than others. Griet learns, for instance, that her family's lack of wealth means that they are less powerful than people like Maria Thins and van Ruijven (see p.169).

Q Does the novel suggest that categories of difference are the only determinants of an individual's power to control their lives and the lives of others? Look, for example, at the portrayal of Catharina.

Q Are these categories of difference more, or less, important to Griet by the end of the novel?

The relationship between men and women

Girl with a Pearl Earring is a thought-provoking tale about the relationships between men and women and the differences between them. It argues that women in the past had less power over their lives than men. The novel is set during a time when girls and women did not own their bodies and their lives, but when they were the possessions first of their parents, then of their employers, and finally of their husbands. As the novel progresses, Griet becomes increasingly aware that she is 'for sale'; she is an object of financial exchange. This disturbing point is made most powerfully through the references to van Baburen's painting, *The Procuress*. The painting depicts an old woman, a procuress, accepting coins from a man in exchange for the favours of a young woman, a prostitute. Looking at the painting upsets Griet: 'The man was smiling at the young woman as if he were squeezing pears in the market to see if they were ripe. I shivered' (p.218). (Remember Pieter's father looks at Griet as if she were a 'plump chicken'.) The painting belongs to Maria Thins, who herself plays the role of 'procuress' in relation to Griet. She organises to sell a painting of her to van Ruijven. The novel makes clear the link between van Ruijven's desire for Griet's body and his demand to have a painting of her. When Griet resists his advances, van Ruijven teases her: 'You'll enjoy it more if you don't fight. And you know, I will have you anyway when I get that painting' (p.214). In effect, van Ruijven gets what we would call a 'pin-up' of Griet. Her efforts to avoid his gaze prove pointless, because in the end he owns an image of her. This relates to the idea that for a woman in Griet's society to hide her face (to look away from men) communicates modesty and innocence, but that to show her face (to meet a man's gaze) suggests that she is another kind of woman. In '1676' we learn that the Vermeers still owe the butchers fifteen guilders. Griet is not amused by her husband's joke that this is the price he paid for her: 'Now I know what a maid is worth' (p.234).

Q Why doesn't Griet laugh when Pieter says this? What does the novel's final sentence mean (p.248; also p.150)?

Q How else does the novel demonstrate that women did not enjoy the same status as men?

Q Does the novel suggest that men had more interesting lives than women? Does the novel end happily for Griet?

The gaze: what it means to 'look' and to 'be looked at'

When Griet first walks away from her parent's home, she is aware that people are watching her as she walks along the street. She is the object of a multiple 'gaze' here and throughout *Girl with a Pearl Earring*. Griet is 'watched curiously' (p.11) from many perspectives: the other main characters, people in her community, the author, herself, anyone who looks at the tile or the painting, readers of the novel. In fact, Chevalier uses the word 'gaze' frequently in the novel, both as a noun and as an adjective. Its frequent appearance in the text points to one of the novel's key themes: what it means to 'look' and to 'be looked at'.

Key point

You can approach this theme from a number of angles: by focusing on the relationship between the gaze and sexual desire; by studying the differences between characters and the ways they look at people and things; by tracing the symbolic significance of 'eyes' in the text; by trying to explain the meaning of Griet's father's blindness; or by considering the novel's take on the relationship between an image and the object or person it represents.

> ***Q*** Look up 'gaze' in a dictionary. What does it mean?

Girl with a Pearl Earring is a sustained exploration of the meaning of 'looking' – at people, at objects, at images. Chevalier uses 'seeing' as a metaphor for 'understanding'. In this novel the verb 'to see' and its synonyms (to look, to gaze, to watch, to glance) have a multitude of meanings and nuances beyond their standard dictionary definition. This is borne out by Chevalier's inclusion of a blind character who can still 'see' images.

> ***Q*** The novel ranks characters according to their capacity to look at people and things carefully. For example, Vermeer is rated more highly than Catharina (see pp.2–3). Rank the other characters in terms of their ability to 'see'.

A great deal of symbolic importance is attached to 'eyes' in this novel. Griet 'sees' emotions in other characters' eyes: e.g. kindness (p.67 and 71), expectation (p.71) and regret (p.228). Chevalier also uses poetic descriptions of eyes to give her characters greater depth and complexity. For example, Tanneke's eyes are 'light blue, as if she had caught the sky in them' (p.16).

> ***Q*** 'I never know what you're thinking, Griet ... You're so calm and quiet, you never say. But there are things inside you. I see them sometimes, hiding in your eyes.' (Pieter the son, p.170) Why do you think eyes are so important in this novel?

We see all of the other characters through Griet's eyes; she studies their appearance and watches their behaviour closely. The detailed physical descriptions of other characters are evidence of this. At the same time, Griet is intensely aware of being watched by the other characters. It is significant that they are all described in terms of how they look at her. She pays attention to their eyes. For example, Pieter the father looks at her as though she were a 'plump chicken he was considering roasting' (p.28). His son's 'eyes came to rest on me like a butterfly on a flower' (p.42). Chevalier uses descriptions of how characters look at each other to illustrate the complex relationships between them. To look at another person is not classified as a simple or innocent thing in this novel. To direct one's gaze at another signifies a number of things in the novel: curiosity, censure, love, desire. Griet feels profoundly uncomfortable being looked at by others. She 'feels' eyes on her at a number of points in the novel. This idea is made even clearer by Griet's physical responses to the gazes of others, especially men. For example, she blushes, shivers, feels hot, and loses her balance when other characters look at her.

Q Why do you think being looked at by men makes Griet so uneasy? Does she respond differently to being looked at by women?

Q 'I thought that you painted what you saw, using the colours you saw. He taught me.' (p.106) Trace the development of Griet's understanding of the relationship between things and 'images' (p.62). What does Vermeer teach her? Did reading this novel improve your understanding of visual perception?

Art/reality and fiction/history

Griet's intense awareness of the gaze of others is crucially important to the meaning of this novel, not least because her story began when its author looked intensely at the painting on the novel's cover. *Girl with a Pearl Earring* invites us both to gaze at the girl who looks out from the painting and to imagine looking through her eyes – to do, that is, what Chevalier did when she wrote the novel. It makes us step back from the fictional story and think about how it was written, to consider what it means to imagine a fictional character living in a specific historical context. Keep in mind that Griet is the only character in Maria Thins' house not inspired by historical records.

Early in the novel, Griet spends time considering the relationship between the painting on the easel (*Woman with a Pearl Necklace*) and the setting for the painting. Here, and throughout the novel, she examines the relationship between things and their images: 'The satin mantle [in the painting] began to look so real I wanted to reach out and touch it' (p.56). There is a fascinating parallel here between what Griet does when she looks at Vermeer's painting and what we do when we read Chevalier's novel (or indeed any historical novel). Like Griet – entranced by the illusion of reality she sees in Vermeer's painting – we become absorbed by Chevalier's moving fictionalisation of history. When I first read this novel, I kept flicking back to look at the cover. I was immediately fascinated by the idea of inventing a history for a girl whose 'real' history has been forgotten or lost. *Girl with a Pearl Earring* encourages us to think about the relationship between realist art and reality, and between historical fiction and history. It does this by inviting us to identify with a character who is herself in the process of learning about the difference between realism and reality, between what looks real and what is real.

Q Remember that reality is not the same thing as realism. Look up these two words in a dictionary or a literary reference text and make notes about the difference between them.

The relationship between Griet and the girl in Vermeer's painting

Girl with a Pearl Earring is a fictional story inspired by a seventeenth-century painting of an unknown girl. We see the painting on the novel's cover before we start reading; it exists both outside the story (in the 'real' world) and in the story (in the 'fictional' world). We sometimes use the word 'extratextual' to refer to things that are outside a text but are relevant to our reading of it. Descriptions of Griet throughout the novel allude to the painting that inspired the novel; they foreshadow how the Vermeer depicted in Chevalier's story will paint her. We are able to recognise these moments (e.g. when Griet sees her reflection in the mirror, when Vermeer sees her washing the windows) because we already know what the actual painting looks like. Chevalier's novel swings back and forth between fiction and history; at times it becomes difficult to tell where the 'truth' ends and make-believe begins.

Griet's father asks her to describe the story in *Young Woman with a Water Pitcher*, but she replies: 'His paintings don't tell stories' (p.97). Her comment invites us to step back from the narrative and to consider the relationship between Chevalier's novel and the painting that inspired it. If Vermeer's paintings don't tell stories, then what are we reading? Chevalier has said that what she sees in Vermeer's paintings is 'stories suggested but not told'. Griet reflects on *Young Woman with a Water Pitcher*: 'It may not have told a story, but it was still a painting you could not stop looking at' (p.97). The painting fuels her imagination (just as *Girl with a Pearl Earring* did Chevalier's), but she cannot be certain about what the young woman in the painting is thinking: 'she's stopped in the middle of what she's doing and is either dreaming or looking at something in the street' (p.96). Her father seeks certainty from the painting: 'you say the girl is doing one thing or maybe another. You're confusing me' (p.97). The point is that Griet enjoys the uncertainty. We can interpret this moment in the novel as a subtle message about the relationship between the book and the painting. Chevalier does not want her novel to become the final word on this evocative painting. She could have told a different story, or many different stories, about the girl and none of them would have been 'true'. The pleasure is in imagining the possibilities.

QUESTIONS & ANSWERS

Essay topics

1 Why does Vermeer leave Griet the pearl earrings?

2 "Van Ruijven had us all – even Maria Thins – running like rabbits before dogs." Is van Ruijven the novel's villain?

3 Pieter the son tells Griet: "But you have little power over what happens to you. Surely you can see that?" Discuss.

4 'Griet's transition from childhood to adulthood is challenging and difficult but rewarding.' Do you agree?

5 "When I made my choice, the choice I knew I had to make, I set my feet carefully along the edge of the point and went the way it told me, walking steadily." How predictable is Griet's decision to marry Pieter?

6 "A maid comes free." What is the significance of the novel's final sentence?

7 '*Girl with a Pearl Earring* shows that individuals' futures are determined by their position in society.' Discuss.

8 '*Girl with a Pearl Earring* illustrates the inequality of men and women.' Discuss.

9 'The text shows that because individuals have to meet the expectations of others they cannot always be true to themselves.' Discuss.

10 '*Girl with a Pearl Earring* shows that the security of the family depends on the financial success of the male breadwinner.' Discuss.

11 Maria Thins repeatedly says, "Never so much trouble with a maid before". Why is Griet such a troublesome maid?

12 How do the paintings featured in *Girl with a Pearl Earring* help to explain one or two important issues in the novel?

Analysing a sample topic

- Your main aim is to develop an argument in response to the question. Try to make the essay topic your own by presenting a strong point of view on the text. Avoid vague responses that try to present too many ideas. A solid, well-supported argument is more important than showing everything you have learnt about the text.
- Support your argument with carefully selected evidence from the text. Remember that your task is to analyse the novel, not to summarise it.
- Watch for contradictions in your argument.
- Plan your essay. Think of your plan as a 'map'. Use it to identify the connections between your paragraphs and to guide you through the essay as you are writing.
- Aim for clear, concise expression. Avoid very long sentences. Choose your words carefully: a simple word is often a better choice than a long, difficult one.

'*Girl with a Pearl Earring* shows that individuals' futures are determined by their position in society.' Discuss.

- Be clear about what you are being asked to discuss. Your first step is to look for the key words in the topic: futures, determined, position in society. Think about synonyms or related words which will help you to write your essay. Making a short list of these at the top of your plan will help you to avoid being too repetitive. It's also a good way to find the subtleties in the topic. A list for this question might look something like this: lives, paths, direction, choice, control, hope, decided, predicted, mapped out, place, role, level of power, wealth, gender, rank, hierarchy, class, trapped, caught.
- Your introduction needs to state your argument and indicate which aspects of the novel your essay focuses on. Try to come up with a strong opening for your essay: use a pertinent quote; or zero in on a moment or scene in the text and then open out to a statement

of your argument. Don't quote the question in your introduction. Aim to be definitive and confident rather than vague and uncertain. Avoid words like 'perhaps', 'seems', and 'possibly'.

- This topic asks you to consider the relationship between the positions key characters hold in Dutch society and what happens to them by the end of the novel. It asks you to measure the level of power individual characters have over the direction of their lives. There are a number of determinants of an individual's rank explored in this novel: gender, wealth, social status (e.g. apothecary versus maid). A good approach would be to focus on Griet and to compare/contrast her with the other characters. Does Griet have a choice in what happens to her, or does she simply follow a predetermined path?
- One way to answer this question would be to argue that a fixed number of possible futures are available to Griet. The 'eight-pointed star' is a key reminder of this throughout the novel. Her choices are limited by her gender, lack of wealth, religion, and low social status. She can remain a maid, become a wife and a mother, or 'become like the maid in the red dress'. She cannot become a property owner like Maria Thins, remain a spoiled child like Catharina, nor – most importantly – can she aspire to be a painter. Make the point that other characters in the novel are similarly restricted by their positions in society. While Griet is allowed a degree of choice, her position in society means that some futures are barred to her: 'I made my choice, the choice I knew I had to make'.
- In the main body of your essay you need to use evidence from the text to demonstrate that it presents a limited number of futures for a girl in Griet's position. Each paragraph should begin with a statement of its main point. For example, 'Griet's gender determines the roles she plays in the novel: maid, model, wife and mother. One exception to this is her role as Vermeer's assistant.' The next step is to explain how this point relates to your key argument. You could say, 'Griet's work in Vermeer's studio allows her – and us – a glimpse of a future that she can never pursue, a future that is made impossible not by a lack of artistic potential but by the place

allowed a woman in her society.' You need to provide evidence from the text to support your claim. For example, in this paragraph focus on moments in the text that show that Griet, in another time and another place, might have been a painter: the vegetable circle, changing the paintings, van Leeuwenhoek's remark, 'Next you'll be teaching her to paint your women for you'. Be sure to explain the relationship between the evidence you cite and the point you're making. In most cases, the end of each paragraph should provide a link to the beginning of the next.

- Other aspects of the text relevant to this question: her family's low economic status; Pieter's 'expectation'; Frans' escape; 'the maid in the red dress'; van Leeuwenhoek's warnings; Griet's relationship with Tanneke; the symbolic significance of the pearl earrings.
- Use your conclusion to wrap up your argument and to reinforce your main points.

SAMPLE ANSWER

Maria Thins repeatedly says, "Never so much trouble with a maid before". Why is Griet such a troublesome maid?

Vermeer's portraits of *The Milkmaid* and *Girl With A Pearl Earring* provide the inspiration for two important and opposing characters in Chevalier's novel: Tanneke and Griet. Both characters work as maids in Vermeer's household and both appear as subjects in his artwork; however, the pair could not be more different in terms of their behaviour, attitudes and work ethic. The contrast between them demonstrates the qualities valued in a maid, and helps to explain why Griet causes 'so much trouble'.

Tanneke prides herself on 'her own industry' and has been a maid for half of her life when Griet arrives at Papists Corner. But Tanneke does not clean the laundry or the floors as well as Griet, and she forgets to put tongue into the meat-safe and was 'never good at roasting'. She is unaware that in order to secure the best cuts one should visit the market early in the day. In all aspects of her work Tanneke is not as thorough nor as diligent as Griet, who gains 'satisfaction' from 'tackling a room in need of a good cleaning'. Yet, Tanneke is considered a superior maid.

Tanneke is less troublesome than Griet because she behaves in the manner expected of a maid. She admires and praises her mistress, and is dutiful and loyal: Griet thinks 'perhaps her loyalty made up for her sloppiness'. Despite the fact that she advises Griet not to listen to Catharina, and appears to have little respect for the 'young mistress', Tanneke risks her own safety to protect Catharina from her crazed brother, Willem. Her selfless behaviour illustrates that a maid's duty is not only to clean the house but to protect it. Tanneke is subservient and selfless, always deferring to the 'wise' Maria Thins and never venturing to think for herself. Ultimately, it is Tanneke's whole-hearted contentment in her role that sets her apart from Griet. Vermeer's portrait *The Milkmaid* is earthy and domestic, depicting a woman with her sleeves rolled up concentrating upon the task of pouring milk into a bowl. In essence, this is Chevalier's Tanneke, too: a woman of uncomplicated emotions and motivations, content to serve.

Griet, conversely, would never be content as a maid: she had 'always wanted to wear pearls'. Griet is 'clever' and feels ashamed of her lowly status. When Tanneke boasts, 'I began [working] when I was fourteen', Griet thinks that she would never have admitted this fact 'with pride'. Griet does not gossip at market, she does not eavesdrop and, aside from cleaning, she does not do the 'things maids are meant to do'. Griet may have found satisfaction in cleaning, but she is too proud to find happiness in servitude.

Griet is independent. She dislikes feeling indebted and is wary of others' expectations. Maria Thins recognises Griet's independence at the outset and advises her to 'keep your thoughts to yourself here'. This does not prevent Griet from thinking and acting according to her own desires. Her wilful streak leads her to keep secrets from Catharina and Tanneke. Griet makes choices: to steal treats for her parents, to assist Vermeer and to wear the earrings offered to her. She thinks and behaves independently, and chooses above all to shape her own destiny.

It is significant that, unlike Tanneke, Griet is not painted as a maid. Rather, her portrait sees her placed alone, as 'neither a lady or a maid' but a woman. The 'trouble' that Griet causes is not due to a lack of thoroughness in her work, but to an aptitude and attitude inappropriate for a social status and her role as a maid. The 'trouble' with Griet is therefore that she possesses the pride, independence and 'cunning' of a 'free' woman.

REFERENCES & READING

Text

Chevalier, Tracy 1999, *Girl with a Pearl Earring*, HarperCollins, London.

Related novels

Maguire, Gregory 1999, *Confessions of an Ugly Stepsister*, ReganBooks, New York. *Only very loosely related to the text.*

Moggach, Deborah 1999, *Tulip Fever*, Heinemann, London. *Includes colour reproductions of paintings by Vermeer and other seventeenth-century Dutch painters.*

Vreeland, Susan 2000, *Girl in Hyacinth Blue*, Penguin, New York.

Weber, Katherine 1998, *The Music Lesson*, Crown Publishers, New York.

Background reading on Vermeer and seventeenth-century Dutch culture

Chevalier acknowledges the following books. They are available through public libraries:

Montias, John Michael 1989, *Vermeer and his Milieu*, Princeton University Press, Princeton, New Jersey.

Schama, Simon 1987, *The Embarrassment of Riches: An Interpretation of Dutch Culture in the Golden Age*, Random House, New York.

Consult encyclopedias and general art history books to learn more.

Articles, interviews and reviews

Grant, Gavin J 2001, 'Interview with Tracy Chevalier', *IndieBound*, http://www.indiebound.org/author-interviews/chevaliertracy

Librie, Felicity 2011, 'Many Voices: An interview with Tracy Chevalier', *Fiction Writers Review*, http://fictionwritersreview.com/interview/many-voices-an-interview-with-tracy-chevalier/

Moggach, Deborah 1999, 'Review of *Girl with a Pearl Earring*', *Tracy Chevalier Online*, originally published by *The Guardian / The Observer*, 7 August, http://www.tchevalier.com/gwape/reviews/guardian.html

Schumacher, Mary Louise 2000, 'Amid our frenzy, an outbreak of quiet, glowing Vermeer,' *Milwaukee Journal Sentinel*, September.

Schwartz, Gary 2001, 'Review', *Art in America*, Volume 89, Issue 3.

Wheelock, Arthur K Jr 1995, 'Vermeer of Delft: His Life and His Ancestry', *Johannes Vermeer*, Exhibition Catalogue, National Gallery of Art, Washington and Royal Cabinet of Paintings Mauritshuis, The Hague, Yale University Press, New Haven and London.

Websites

Official website of *Girl With a Pearl Earring*: http://www.tchevalier.com/gwape/index.html
Includes information about Chevalier, links to interviews with her and to reviews of the novel, background information about Vermeer, and information about the paintings mentioned in the novel.

Official website of Tracy Chevalier: http://www.tchevalier.com

View Vermeer's complete works online: http://www.essentialvermeer.com/